WOMEN
& MONEY

OWNING THE POWER TO CONTROL YOUR DESTINY

SUZE ORMAN

SPIEGEL & GRAU
NEW YORK
2007

PRINTED IN THE UNITED STATES OF AMERICA

SPIEGEL & GRAU and its logo are trademarks of Random House, Inc.

Visit our website at www.spiegelandgrau.com

Book design by Chris Welch

Cataloging-in-Publication Data is on file with the Library of Congress.

ISBN 978-0-385-51931-1

1 3 5 7 9 10 8 6 4 2

First Edition

This book is dedicated to all the women of yesterday, today, and tomorrow. May we always support one another and wish each other greatness.

CONTENTS

Saxon Hotel, Johannesburg, South Africa, November 2005. I was about to leave my hotel suite to go on a safari with two of my closest friends in life when the phone rang. We all wondered who in the world could be calling us, since hardly anyone knew that we were in South Africa, let alone where we were staying. It was Julie Grau, my editor and publisher for *The Courage to Be Rich, The Road to Wealth, The Ask Suze Library Series,* and *The Money Book for the Young, Fabulous & Broke.* She sounded a little shaky and said that she had something she needed to tell me. After careful contemplation, she and her co-publisher Cindy Spiegel had decided to leave their current place of employment to start a new division within the Doubleday Publishing Group of Random House, Inc. Julie wanted me to hear this news from her rather than read about it in the paper or hear it from someone else.

Despite the fact that her leaving would affect me as well, I was ecstatic. Finally, Julie was taking action in a way that would allow her to control her destiny. For years Julie and I had talked on the phone about money; I've always wanted her to get more involved with it, learn how to invest it, care about it, and ask for more for herself. But my efforts always seemed in vain. Like so many women, Julie was too busy making money for other people to take the time to make more out of the money she was making for herself.

When I would hang up after one of these conversations, I would always think, if only she really understood how incredible she is. If only Julie saw in herself what I saw in her. If only Julie understood that she was worth so much more. Those are the very things that I want all women to see in themselves. But now, I had to give her credit; she decided she had to leave in order to value herself. I knew that leaving the publishing house she had helped to establish was not easy for her; it is never easy to leave that which is familiar and safe to go on to something new and unknown, especially for a woman. For a woman, a working family is more important than money. (I have to say that I find it fascinating that this change came when Julie was four months pregnant. It was almost as if she couldn't take these actions when she was on her own, but now that she had a new family it was almost as if she couldn't afford *not* to do it for them. But again, that is what women do, is it not? They do for others what they cannot do for themselves.)

When I asked Julie the name of her new publishing division, she told me she didn't know yet, but she and Cindy were fiddling around with some ideas. People suggested that they name their company Spiegel & Grau (their last names), and she would reply, "Are you kidding? No way. It's about the books. It's not about us." Another typical response from a woman, don't you think? Well, after some time Julie started to get in touch with her own power, and she and Cindy decided to put their names on their new company. This was a huge step for Julie as it is for any woman when she starts to understand the power of saying her name.

Obviously I decided to follow Julie to her new company, and I am proud to say that she is once again my publisher and editor. I am greatly honored that mine is the first book to be published by Spiegel & Grau. That this book's title is *Women & Money,* and its themes are echoed in the story you are about to read, makes it even more special to me.

Usually at the beginning of my books I have a long list of the people, some I've worked with for years and some who have just come aboard, to thank for all they have done to help me become who I am today. You all know who you are, and I hope you can feel that, in my own way, I thank you every day. I thank you in my prayers and wishes, as well as when I speak or write to you. So I give you all one great group acknowledgment, and I hope you understand that this time there is only one woman that I want to acknowledge by name, and that is Julie, who has looked at almost every word I have ever written, edited it, guided it, and, when needed, made it better. For those of you reading this, I want you to know that there is a little bit of every woman in Julie. She is a wife, a daughter, a mom, a stepmom, a boss, an employee, a best friend, a volunteer, an aunt, a niece, and a sister, all in one. She has a husband, Adam, and is the proud legal mother now of his ten-year-old son, Jackson. Last year Julie gave birth to a son, Rian, whom everyone for some reason calls Beanie. She did all this at the same time this book was being born. I have watched in amazement and with the utmost respect as Julie keeps it all going—from being a new mother, to starting a new company, to editing my book, to signing up new authors, to hiring employees, and going to meeting after meeting, even as she runs uptown to dress up for Halloween with Jackson, and goes to dinner at her mom's, and is home on Friday nights in time to light candles for the Sabbath. I have watched her do it all with grace, humility, love, and compassion. I have watched her be the perfect representative for all of us women.

So my dear Julie—for this, your first book in your new publishing house, for your new sons, your new work, your family, your friends, and for bringing new meaning to the words "valuing yourself"—I acknowledge your efforts. I acknowledge your incredible generosity, your courage, your wisdom, your beauty, and our friendship.

May this book be the start of a list of successes for you, my friend, and may we forever remember what is possible in life when we choose to own the power to control our destinies. We have come a long way, my dear Jules, and I am so glad we did.

With all my love and respect,
Suze

WOMEN
& MONEY

1

FOR WOMEN ONLY

I never thought I'd write a book about money just for women. I never thought it was necessary. So then why am I doing just that in my eighth book? And why now? Let me explain.

All my previous books were written with the belief that gender is not a factor on any level in mastering the nuts and bolts of smart financial management. Women can invest, save, and handle debt just as well and skillfully as any man. I still believe that— why would anyone think differently?

So imagine my surprise when I learned that some of the people closest to me in my life were in the dark about their own finances. Clueless. Or, in some cases, willfully resisting doing what they knew needed to be done. I'm talking about smart, competent, accomplished women who present a face to the world that is pure confidence and capability. Do you mean to tell me that I, Suze Orman, who make my living solving the financial problems of total strangers, couldn't spot the trouble brewing so close to home? I don't think I'm blind; I just think that these women became very, very good at hiding their troubles from me. Why not? They had years of practice hiding them from themselves.

Frankly, I was shocked. It was a real reckoning. It began with a friend, a very high-powered businesswoman who handles millions and millions of dollars a year, who refused to sign will and trust documents I'd helped her to prepare. I can't tell you why, but those papers sat on her desk for *three years*—she clearly had some kind of block that prevented her from simply signing her name and having the documents notarized. Even as I write, she has still not completed them. Then another friend, a woman with some amazing professional credits under her belt, broke down and confessed that she had rung up such staggering bills over the years that she was too terrified to tell anyone and had no idea how to pay them off. Not long after, I heard from yet another friend who finally woke up to the fact that her employer was paying her significantly less than every other executive of comparable rank in her company. Her division was one of the most profitable and consistent earners for the company, but still she just accepted the minimal increases her boss would hand her every year at review time. And even now, out of some misguided loyalty, she was reluctant to leave the employer that took advantage of her year after year.

What was going on here?

Upon further investigation, I learned that so many women in my life—friends, acquaintances, readers, people from my TV audience—all had this stumbling block in common: an "unknown factor" that prevented them from doing the right thing with their money. Maybe it was fear of the unknown for some; maybe for others it was a little streak of rebellion for holding it together in every other part of their lives; or maybe it was just that they felt that things had gotten so far out of hand, they were embarrassed to ask for help and reveal just how much they didn't know.

Women have been thrust into an entirely new relationship with money that is profoundly different from anything we have ever encountered before. The shifting roles of women at home and at work have dramatically changed where and how money interacts with a woman's life. Yet what I see is that while women have established or expanded their roles and relationships, when it comes to navigating the financial ramifications of this new world, they are using old maps that don't get them where they really want and need to go.

It doesn't matter if I am in a room full of business executives or stay-at-home moms, I find the core problem to be universal: When it comes to making decisions with money, you refuse to own your power, to act in *your* best interest. It is not a question of intelligence; you absolutely have what it takes to understand what you should be doing. But you simply won't bring yourself to take care of yourself financially, especially if those actions compete with taking care of those you love. Your inner nurturer reigns supreme; you do for everyone before you do for yourself.

No matter how good your intentions may be, they are nonetheless draining you.

So that is why my eighth book is called *Women & Money*.

The challenge is to finally learn—and accept—that to be truly powerful in your life requires making money moves that work for you. Now, I am not suggesting you replace nurturer with narcissist. I do not want you to discard your generosity or shed your supportive and kind nature. This book is not about becoming more by becoming more selfish. Far from it. I simply want you to give *to* yourself as much as you give *of* yourself. By taking care of yourself financially, you will truly be able to take care of those you love.

Becoming powerful in a lasting, beneficial way is never done at the expense of others; it is done for the good of all. Women are the bedrock of their families, of their communities—so many are dependent on us. If we stand strong and know who we are and what we can create, we will easily be able to hold up those we love and those who need a helping hand.

Please know that there is not one sentence of blame within these pages. I appreciate that the incredible multitasking job called *your life* makes it hard, if not impossible, to find the time, energy, or desire to pay attention to what you are doing wrong with your money, let alone figure out what is the right thing to do. Your kids need mothering, your partner needs loving, your parents need help, your career needs your energy, and your friends need your ear. Throw into that mix the dry cleaning that needs to be picked up, the groceries that need to be bought, the meals that need to be prepared, and the house that needs to be cleaned, and it's no surprise that anything to do with money takes a backseat.

The aim of this book is to make this transformation as easy as possible.

In order to do that, I'm going to help you toward an understanding of how we got here—why we undermine ourselves and why deciding to seize control over our financial lives is, in fact, a groundbreaking, trailblazing decision. I also hope I can provide you with the motivation to *want* to act, to tackle these challenges head-on and own your power.

I'll provide you with the guidance and pragmatic tools to feel secure and in control of your financial life as quickly and as painlessly as possible. To that end, I've come up with a five-month course of action that I've named **The Save Yourself Plan** to help you over the blocks and set you up for a lifetime of financial security. I've tried to pinpoint why it is that other books have failed you, why your moments of resolve and inspiration inevitably lost their steam and were short-lived. I've taken a realistic approach and come up with a strategy that anticipates the fatigue and fear and lack of determination and is designed to keep you engaged, educate you, and—can you believe it?—inspire you to want to do more. I will not overwhelm you with laundry lists of seemingly insurmountable chores. I've identified core tasks—and made them as comprehensive and easy to follow as possible. It is my goal that, at the end of five months, you will be able to chart your progress and feel the pride and relief that come with being in control of a part of your life that has, until now, remained outside your grasp.

And finally, I hope this book will point you toward the future and inspire you, show you what is possible not just for our generation but for generations to come.

Because this is truly the best part: These life-altering changes are an amazing legacy, a gift to every daughter and granddaughter—those who grace your life today and those yet to be born.

Now you know why I truly believe that this book—the one I never planned to write, the one for women only—is the most important book I have ever written.

2

IMAGINE WHAT'S
POSSIBLE

A book with the title *Women & Money* must begin with the story of how far women have come financially in the past three decades. It's not only a remarkable tale of social progress, it's a reminder for us that changes that take place on a personal level, every day, in small doses, add up to dramatic societal and cultural shifts over time.

Women today make up nearly half of the total workforce in this country. Over the past thirty years, women's income has soared a dramatic 63 percent. Forty-nine percent of all professional- and managerial-level workers are women. Women bring in half or more of the income in the majority of U.S. households—a growing trend that made the cover of *Newsweek* and was front-page news in many of the nation's newspapers. Women-owned businesses comprise 40 percent of all companies in the United States. There are more women than ever before who can count themselves among the country's millionaires, more women in upper management, and more women in positions of power in the government.

We have a right to be proud of our progress. I am so honored to witness this revolution in my lifetime. I only wish it told the whole truth.

Now, would you like to hear the other side of the story? Ninety percent of women who participated in a 2006 survey commissioned by Allianz Insurance rated themselves as feeling insecure when it came to their finances. *Ninety* percent! In the same survey, *nearly half* the respondents said that the prospect of ending up a bag lady has crossed their minds. A 2006 Prudential financial poll found that only 1 percent of the women surveyed gave themselves an A in rating their knowledge of financial products and services. Two-thirds of women have not talked with their husbands about such things as life insurance and preparing a will. Nearly 80 percent of women said they would depend on Social Security in their golden years. Did you know that women are nearly twice as likely as men to retire in poverty?

For years now, I have been in the privileged position of talking to thousands and thousands of women a year—from the callers to my TV show, to those who come to hear me speak, to those who write me e-mails on my website, to my very own friends and family. So I hear, see, and feel your fears, insecurities, and troubles, very often firsthand, and I have come face-to-face with this painful truth: For all the advancements women have made in the last thirty, forty years—and without a doubt they are remarkable accomplishments—I am stunned by how little has really changed in the way women deal with money. There are huge disconnects in play here—between what we know and how we act; between what we think and what we say; between our ability as achievers and our financial underachieving; between how we present ourselves to the world and how we really feel about ourselves inside; between what we deserve in our lives and what we resign ourselves to; between the power we have within reach and the powerlessness that rules our actions.

In 1980, when I was hired as a financial advisor for Merrill Lynch, I was one of the few women in the Oakland, California, office. In the eyes of my (male) boss, that made me the perfect candidate to work with all the women who walked through the door. Back then, women who came to a brokerage firm looking for financial advice had, for the most part, either inherited money, received it in a divorce, been widowed, or were suddenly thrust into a position of helping their parents handle their money. In only a few instances had women come in with money they'd made on their own. No matter the circumstances that brought them to the brokerage firm, they all had the same reason for being there: They did not want the responsibility of managing their money. I always felt they hired me simply to babysit their money for them.

More than twenty-five years later, the story is much the same. Regardless of the gains in our financial status, I know and you know that women still don't want to take responsibility when it comes to their money. Yes, women are making more money than ever before, but they are not making more of what they make. What do I mean by that? Your retirement money sits in cash because you haven't figured out how to invest it properly, so you do nothing. You've convinced yourself that you'll be working forever, so the value of each paycheck becomes meaningless—after all, there will always be another one. Your closet houses the wardrobe of a powerful and stylish woman, but the dirty secret is that your credit cards are maxed out and you don't know how you're going to pay them off. But it's not just about saving and investing. It's about not asking for a raise at work when you know you are being undervalued. It's about the fear and loathing you feel when it's time to pay the bills every month because you don't know exactly what you have, where it's going, and why there isn't more left when it's all said and done. It's about how you berate yourself all the time for not knowing more and doing more . . . yet stay resigned to this feeling of helplessness and despair as time ticks away.

This problem, in my opinion, is enormous and pervasive and universal. It crosses all ages, all races, all tax brackets. Who can deny the fact that there is a fundamental block at work here that is preventing women from becoming as powerful as they are meant to be? Not me. I would be the first one to tell you that everything you need to know to secure your financial future, to educate yourself, to make your life easy—it's all out there. Yours for the asking. But you don't ask; you don't want to know.

I see this fundamental denial, this resistance in all women, no matter what they do, how they live, or where they are in their lives. I see you literally giving your money away rather than dealing with it. I see stay-at-home moms who work twenty-four hours a day and yet hand over all power and control to their husbands because they don't earn the money. I see successful single women who refuse to focus on what they need to do today to ensure their financial security years from now. I see women in second marriages who fail to protect the assets they accumulated before they remarried and feel uncomfortable bringing up money issues with their new husbands. I see divorced women of all ages who go into full-blown panic mode when faced with the reality that they have no clue what money exists, what to do when they get their share of the settlement, and whether they will be able to maintain their lifestyle post-divorce. And the most heartbreaking of them all? I hear older women use words like "powerless" and "worthless" to describe themselves. These women are filled with regret when it comes to the way they've lived their financial lives.

So why do you all do this to yourselves? Why are you voluntarily committing financial suicide, and doing it with a smile on your face?

Let me put it another way. Ask yourself this:

Why is it that women, who are so competent in all other areas of their lives, cannot find the same competence when it comes to matters of money?

I have asked this question—of myself and others—over and over. Of course, there is no one answer. After much contemplation, here is what I have come up with:

The matter of women and money is clearly a complicated issue that has much to do with our history and traditions, both societal and familial. These deep-seated issues are major hurdles to overcome, major tides to turn—and that doesn't happen overnight. It can take generations to effect change of this magnitude in our daily behavior. We'll explore these issues in greater depth in the chapters ahead, because they are absolutely a root cause of this problem. But we'll have to look at this on a behavioral level, too, since traits that are fundamental to our nature clearly affect how we approach money as well.

Consider this: It's a generally accepted belief that nurturing comes as a basic instinct to women. We give of ourselves; we take care of our family, our friends, our colleagues. It's in our nature to nurture. So why don't we take care of our money? Why don't we want to take care of our money as well as we take care of the spouses, partners, children, pets, plants, and whatever else is in our lives that we love and cherish?

I want you to think about that question. The answer is critical to uncovering what is at work here and what is holding you back. So I'll ask it again:

Why don't we show our money the same care and attention that we shower on every other important relationship in our lives?

Because we don't have a relationship with our money.

Correction: We do have a relationship with our money. It's just a totally dysfunctional one.

Let me tell you why I say this. Across the board, I see women refusing to engage with their money until they are forced to—because of the birth of children, or divorce, or death, for example. In other words, we do not relate to it until we are in extreme, life-changing situations in which we have no choice but to confront money matters. Until then, we don't apply that same primal, nurturing impulse when it comes to taking care of our money—and by extension, *ourselves*. We can't even accept this as a fact—that **our money is indeed an extension of ourselves.** Instead, we persist in a dysfunctional relationship—we ignore our money, deny its needs, we are afraid of it, afraid of failing, afraid it will expose our shortcomings, which leads to shame. What do we do with all these uncomfortable feelings? We suppress them, we put them away, we don't deal with them. It becomes far easier to ignore the money issue altogether. And the longer we ignore it, the worse the situation becomes; we grow even more fearful as time passes that it's too late for us to learn, too late to even try. So we give up. Who likes a failed relationship? Nobody. Better to have no relationship at all than a failed one. . . .

But money is not a person you can write out of your life. You need money to live.

So then let's turn this relationship theory around and ask ourselves the following question: In order to become competent and successful in handling our money, in order to become the fully responsible women we know we should be, what does that require of us?

We have to develop a healthy, honest relationship with our money. And we have to see this relationship as a reflection of our relationship with ourselves.

I can't put it any more simply or emphatically: How we behave toward our money, how we treat our money, speaks volumes about how we perceive and value ourselves. If we aren't powerful with money, we aren't powerful period. What is at stake here is not just money—it's far bigger. This is about your sense of who you are and what you deserve. Lasting net worth comes only when you have a healthy and strong sense of self-worth. And right now, the money disconnect, this dysfunctional relationship, is a barrier to both.

Once you fully appreciate this and hold it as an absolute truth, you will also understand that your destiny depends on the health of this relationship. Are you honestly prepared to roll the dice on this one, or would you rather feel that you have the ability, the determination, the power to make this relationship work—as surely as you know how to nurture and give care to all the people you love in your life?

How do you repair this relationship?

The same way you would repair any relationship that is damaged: by acknowledging your mistakes, taking responsibility, and resolving to act in a way that will bring about change for the better. In the case of you and your money, that means making strong money moves, moves with the goal of making you feel more powerful and secure. If you show money the respect it deserves today and carry it through in all your actions, then one day, when you can no longer take care of it, your money will take care of you. Respecting your relationship with money, you see, is the key not only to your security and independence, but to your happiness, as well.

Now let's talk about happiness for a moment.

The simple fact is that **nothing more directly affects your happiness than money.**

Oh, I know, some of you are just horrified by this notion, maybe even offended. *Suze, how could you?!* Happiness is about all the things money can't buy—health, love, respect—right? Absolutely true—all of these are essential to a happy life. All are determined by who you are and not what you have. But the kind of happiness

I am talking about is your quality of life—the ability to enjoy life, to live life to its fullest potential. And I challenge anyone to tell me that such things aren't factors in your overall happiness.

Let's just walk through this together for a moment. Yes, I know that your health and the health of your loved ones is paramount, but explain to me what would happen if, God forbid, any one of you fell ill. Wouldn't you want the best care that money can buy? Wouldn't you be grateful that you were in a good health plan? And isn't it money that puts the roof over your head, and money that allows you to move to a neighborhood with a great public school system? And money that allows you to retire early, or quit your job while you go back to school to pursue a new career?

So why is it, then, that we are so reluctant to embrace this concept fully—that money is a factor in determining our happiness? Why is it that in a recent survey called "Authentic Happiness" there was not a single question or answer that contained the word *money*? What bothers me about this is that I think it's a lie not to acknowledge the power money has to make our lives better and happier. It's not a subject for polite company? Is that what you've been raised to believe? Well, I'm here to tell you that this isn't just a problem of semantics. I believe that this "conspiracy of silence" is another reason why so many women are in the dark about financial matters. I have often said that we must be careful of our words, for words become actions. Well, the opposite of that is true, too: Silence leads to inaction. We don't talk about money with our friends, our parents, our children—and that's where we get in trouble. How are we supposed to teach our children, how are we supposed to educate ourselves, if there isn't a free and frank flow of information about money? Why do we behave so carelessly with our money? Would we do that if we believed our very happiness depended on it? Let me put it this way: If we persist in denying money its place in our lives, if we don't give it the respect it most certainly deserves, then it will surely lead to unhappiness.

What you really have to understand and believe is that every one of you already has more than what it takes to own the power to control your financial destiny. I am asking you now to harness the incredible intelligence and competence that serve you so well in so many other aspects of your life and apply it to your money. Anyone who has it in them to run a household, run a company, run a department of a company, run a car pool, or run a marathon is fully equipped to take control here. Anyone who is a supportive and caring wife, partner, mother, sister, daughter, best friend, caretaker, aunt, grandmother, or colleague has all the skills necessary to forge a solid relationship with her money and to make the kind of smart money choices that support you rather than sabotage you. **That's what controlling your financial destiny comes down to: knowing what to do and what not to do—and having the conviction and confidence to go out and do it. Not just think about it. Or intend to do it next week or next month. To actually do it. Right now.**

Make that commitment to yourself first, and I will help you. And together, let's imagine what's possible when you do:

Imagine: Opening the credit card bill each month and knowing you will be able to pay it off.

Imagine: Knowing you have done everything to take care of your family if something happens to you.

Imagine: Staying in a relationship purely for love, not because you have no idea how you would make it financially on your own.

Imagine: Loving yourself enough to choose a partner you don't have to rescue.

Imagine: Owning your home outright. No more mortgage payments. No one can ever take it away from you.

Imagine: Knowing you will be able to retire comfortably one day.

Imagine: Raising children who've learned from you the wisdom of living within your means, rather than living out of control.

Imagine: Knowing you have helped your parents live full lives, without fear or uncertainty, right to the end.

The payoff for your commitment extends beyond your finances. Having a healthy relationship with money puts you in a position to have better relationships with everyone in your life. It all flows together. A woman who is more financially confident and secure is a happier woman. And a happier woman is going to be better able to nurture, share, and give support to all those in her life.
All of it is possible.

YOUR OWN RICH LIFE: AN EXERCISE

My friend Allee Willis is a composer of hit songs. She has the creative life we all dream of—her work is her passion, her passion is her work. She has built a life that is devoted to nurturing her creativity, and she finds inspiration in the everyday. Down to the very last pencil in her home, she will tell you, everything is designed to inspire and delight her senses; she has a holistic and integrative approach to living. And yet there was one area of her life that she viewed as separate and foreign: her finances. She and I have corresponded a lot over the past year. A recent Broadway success, *The Color Purple,* forced her to take stock of what she had and, thankfully, make way for more. "Financially I'm at a standstill," she wrote me last year. "I used to think that my reluctance to handle money was based on fear, but I realized that I can't do anything unless my heart is in it. Which is very hard to accomplish without my brain being in it, too. If I understood more, I would become passionate about money management and then I wouldn't view it as a separate and foreign area of my life. Once I enjoy something, it becomes part of the bigger creative and whole-self picture, and then it's easy for me to remain active, interested, and enthusiastic."

I responded to Allee with some tough love: I pointed out that she nurtured projects until they were successful and then took her paychecks and wasted them on unnecessary objects, vacations, and other people. Taking care of the world, just because she can. It was time for her to get rid of all the junk in her life and focus on the things that would bring her long-term security. I gave it to her good—but she gave it back to me even better.

Allee accused me of not understanding her definition of what it means to be rich and not being sympathetic enough to the struggles of creative souls like her. She defended the environment she created as one that enriches her visually, aesthetically, and spiritually—an absolute necessity for an artist's state of mind. "Rich means different things to different people," she wrote. "Financial security is your lifeblood. Creative freedom and expression is mine. If you can experience life in all its forms and experience that you are one with it, then you are the richest person in the world. And when one is in tune with this and one knows the value of material things in creating that environment, the senses are in high creative alert all the time. I know—*financial security makes all of this better*. I have at least five copies of *The 9 Steps to Financial Freedom* bought five separate times because I was tired of feeling frustrated, embarrassed, and scared that I didn't have my financial life together. In a burst of 'I can do it!' I'd read the book. But taking the steps to turn things around once the security of reading the book was over proved too much to overcome. You need to speak to me from a place where you understand how people like me function. I need you to see the merits of incorporating my way into yours."

I took her words to heart every time I sat down to write more of this book, for she articulated the mission of it—to inspire readers to action by speaking from a place of understanding.

One week later, I got a surprising e-mail from Allee. "I took a huge step last week right after I e-mailed you," she wrote. She moved money into accounts that paid more interest. She paid off a big chunk of her mortgage. She had a good long meeting with her accountant. "Between reading your books and mulling all this over, I understood every single word that was spoken. So I'm on the move finally! But it was writing you that e-mail about what real wealth means to me that was the main instigator to my finally taking action. I love my life and want to live it even more, which the financial gains will allow."

Allee's circumstances are unique, and she is without a doubt very blessed and fortunate. But I wanted to share her story—and her process—with you because I was surprised and fascinated by what finally moved her to act. The exercise of articulating what she valued most in her life was the most powerful motivator of all. I'd like you to find a few quiet moments and write your own definition of a rich life. Remind yourself what it is you love about your life—and how you wish you could live it more fully. Articulate for yourself that which you cherish. I believe that somewhere in those lines you will find your own personal motivation to learn and act and achieve the destiny I am asking you to dare to imagine for yourself.

3

NO SHAME,
NO BLAME

In order to build a healthy relationship with money, there are some attitudes I am going to ask you to cast off—forever. First among them are two of the heaviest weights women carry, invisible twin obstacles of our past: the burden of shame and the tendency to blame.

You don't feel confident in your knowledge of how money works, so you hide behind the shame of it, deferring decisions to others or staying stuck in a pattern of inaction. You wrap yourself in the cloak of shame rather than reveal your shortcomings—you, after all, are a doer! You have to be all things to all people—mother, wife, dutiful daughter, supportive friend, school volunteer, cheerleader at home and at work. No room to betray uncertainty in that picture! No time to learn anyway—*who has the time?!* You're so busy. And besides, you tell yourself, I probably should have learned that ages ago. When did everybody else learn this and not you? Hmm, maybe you were absent that day. . . . At this point, it's simply too embarrassing to reveal the depths of what you do not know.

And where the mantle of shame stops, the tendency to blame kicks in. *It's not my fault!* you tell me. (a) Society (b) My parents (c) My husband/ex-husband (d) All of the above . . . held me back! Where were the role models? No one taught me, no one showed me how, money decisions were always made for me. Now, I'm not belittling these factors or making fun of you. There's a lot of legitimacy in these complaints. Long-standing traditions in society and in the home have not made it easy for women to get the financial education they need to become competent, informed participants in their own affairs. Even today, no one is going to hand it to you—you have to go get it for yourself. It amazes me that a person can go through twelve years of school, four years of college, and then on to graduate study, and nowhere along the way were they required to take a single class on personal finance.

But let me ask you this: Where does blame get you? The answer is *nowhere*. **Blame renders you powerless.** You must get past blame to become who you are meant to be. And what does shame do to you? **Shame only serves to hold you back.** This book is about facing forward, not staying stuck in the past. It is fine to understand how we got here, but the next breath must contain a resolve to move ahead into a future that looks entirely different, into a destiny that is all yours. I want you to use your past to propel you into your future, rather than keep you in the dark of what no longer exists.

Easy for you to say, Suze. Is that what you're thinking? Are you wondering how I could possibly know about your situation? After all, I'm rich! I have everything I need, everything I want. You're right—I'm rich. But that was not always the case. Do you think I was raised in a family that had money and paid for a fabulous education? Did you think I had an MBA from some fancy business school? Nothing could be further from the truth. Maybe you think I married money. Not true—in fact, I never got married (which is probably why I have money today!). Let me tell you where I came from and how I got here—so you will under-stand that there is no excuse, no amount of shame or blame, that can hold you back and keep you from becoming all you are meant to be and having all that you deserve.

SUZE'S STORY

When I was a little girl, I had a speech impediment. I couldn't pronounce my *r*'s, *s*'s, or *t*'s properly, so words such as "beautiful," for example, came out as "boobital." To this day, if you listen closely when I speak, you can still hear it. Words like "fear" and "fair" and "bear" and "beer" sound the same, and a word like "shouldn't" comes out sounding like "shunt." Back then, because I couldn't speak well, I also couldn't read very well. In grammar school on the South Side of Chicago, I had to take reading exams, and would always score among the lowest in the class. One year a teacher decided that he would seat us according to our reading scores. There were my three best friends in the first three seats of the first row, while I was banished to the last seat in the sixth row. If I always secretly felt dumb, it was now officially confirmed for everyone to see. Talk about feeling ashamed.

This feeling that I couldn't make it scholastically continued to haunt me throughout high school and on into college. I knew I would never amount to anything, so why even bother to try? Nevertheless, in my family and in the families of my friends, it was a given that we'd all go to college. In my case, I knew that I would have to pay for college myself, because my parents were having a hard time with money. The only options for me were community college or a state school. I applied to the University of Illinois at Urbana-Champaign and to my amazement, even though I did not score well on my SATs, I was accepted. When I arrived, I met with a guidance counselor who asked me what I wanted to study. I told him that I wanted to become a brain surgeon. He looked at my grades and said, "I don't think so. You don't have what it takes. Why not try something easier?" I did a little investigation and found out that the easiest major was social work, so I signed up for that. Why not take the easy way out? Why try harder?

During my first year at the University of Illinois, I lived in the Florida Avenue Residences in room 222 and worked in the dormitory's dish room seven days a week to pay the bills. In my second year, I shared a one-bedroom apartment off campus with two friends I had met in the dorm, Carole Morgan and Judy Jacklin. Judy had a hilarious boyfriend named John Belushi, and the four of us had quite the adventure for the next three years. (Yes, this is the very same John Belushi who went on to superstardom on *Saturday Night Live*. Judy and John got married and the rest is history, but that's a story for another book.)

I was supposed to graduate in 1973, but my degree was withheld because I hadn't fulfilled the language requirement. Once again, it was the shame of my grade-school years holding me back. If I had trouble with English, what made me think I could learn a foreign language? I decided to leave school without my degree. I wanted to see America. I wanted to see what a hill looked like . . . a mountain . . . the Grand Canyon!

I borrowed $1,500 from my brother to buy a Ford Econoline van and, with the help of my friend Mary Corlin (a great friend to this day), converted the van into a place I could sleep during the drive across country. I convinced three friends—Laurie, Sherry, and Vicky—to come with me; I was way too scared to try this on my own. With $300 and a converted van to my name, we set out to see America. Sherry and Vicky jumped out in Los Angeles, but Laurie and I continued on to Berkeley, California. As we drove through the hills on the day of our arrival, we were stopped by a man with a red flag who held up traffic so trees that had been cut down could be cleared. That year a frost in the Berkeley Hills killed many of the eucalyptus trees. I got out of the van to watch and walked up to the man with the red flag and asked him if they needed any help. He pointed me to the boss, and before we knew it Laurie and I had landed our first jobs—working for Coley Tree Service for $3.50 an hour. We worked as tree clearers for two months, living out of the van and using a friend's home nearby to shower.

When it was time to move on, I applied for a job as a waitress at the Buttercup Bakery, a great little place where we used to get our coffee. To my delight, I got the job. While I worked at the Buttercup, I faced up to my shame of not having finished college and took Spanish classes at Hayward State University. Finally, in 1976, I got my degree from the University of Illinois. I was an official college graduate, working as a waitress. I stayed at the Buttercup Bakery, where I made about $400 a month, until 1980, when I was twenty-nine years old. (Let me do the math for you. Yes, it's true, I am fifty-five.)

After six years of waitressing, I had this thought that I could be more than just a waitress. I wanted to own my own restaurant. I called up my parents and asked to borrow $20,000. My mom said, "Honey, where do you expect us to come up with this? We don't have that kind of money to give you." I should have known better than to ask for something I knew my parents didn't have to give away. There's nothing a parent wants more than to help a child realize a dream; I knew my mother would have done anything to help me, but she was powerless. I felt awful.

The next day at work, a man I had been waiting on for six years, Fred Hasbrook, noticed that I wasn't my usual cheerful self. "What's wrong, sunshine? You don't look happy," he said. I told Fred about having asked my parents for a $20,000 loan. Fred ate his breakfast and then talked to some of the other customers I'd been waiting on all those years. Before he left the restaurant, he came up to the counter and handed me a personal check for $2,000, a bunch of other checks and commitments from the other customers that totaled $50,000, and a note that read: THIS IS FOR PEOPLE LIKE YOU, SO THAT YOUR DREAMS CAN COME TRUE. TO BE PAID BACK IN TEN YEARS, IF YOU CAN, WITH NO INTEREST. I couldn't believe my eyes.

"I have to ask you a question," I said to Fred. "Are these checks going to bounce like all of mine do?"

"No, Suze," he said. "What I want you to do is to put this in a money market account at Merrill Lynch until you've raised enough money to open your restaurant."

"Fred," I said, "what is Merrill Lynch and what is a money market account?"

After a brief tutorial from Fred, I went to the Oakland office of Merrill Lynch to deposit the money. I was assigned to the broker of the day—the one who handled all the walk-in clients that day. My broker was named Randy. I told Randy the story of how I had come by this money and that it needed to stay safe and sound. I told Randy that I made only $400 a month as a waitress and that I needed to raise more money in order to open up my own business. He looked at me and said, "Suze, how would you like to make a quick hundred dollars a week?"

"You bet," I said. "That's about what I make as a waitress."

"Just sign here on the dotted line and we'll see what we can do," he said. I did exactly what he asked, never thinking that it was stupid or dangerous for me to sign blank papers. Randy worked for Merrill Lynch, after all, and Fred said it was a great place to do business.

(Now, before I go any further, I just want to say that this is not a commentary on Merrill Lynch. Merrill Lynch is a fine, upstanding, and honest brokerage firm, but the bosses in the Oakland office had hired someone who didn't uphold their standards. If you have an account with Merrill or want to open up an account with Merrill, go right ahead; this particular bad seed is long gone. But more on that later. . . .)

It turned out that after I left that day, Randy had filled out the papers I had signed to make it look as if I could afford to risk the money I had deposited into the Merrill Lynch account. He got me into one of the more speculative investing strategies—buying options. At first, I was making great money. I was amazed. I found the perfect location for my restaurant and was having plans drawn up by an architect. My dream was within reach. Other people believed in me and lent me more money. We were off and running—that is, until the markets turned. Within three months, I'd lost all the money in the account. All of it. I didn't know what to do. I knew I owed a lot of money, and I knew I had no way to pay it back. I was still making only $400 a month!

During this time, I had been following what Randy was doing and was trying to learn as much as possible. I watched *Wall Street Week* on PBS every Friday night, I read *Barron's* and the *Wall Street Journal*. I taped the pages with the stock and option prices to my bedroom walls. After all the money was lost, I said to myself, "Hey, if Randy can be a broker, I can be a broker, too— after all, it seems like they just make people broker!" I got dressed in my best red-and-white-striped Sassoon pants, tucked them into my white cowboy boots, and put on a blue silk top. I thought I looked great! So did my friends at the Buttercup, who wished me luck as I set off for my job interview to become a stockbroker at the very office that had lost me all my money.

Five men interviewed me that day, and all of them asked me why I had dressed that way. I told them I didn't know I wasn't supposed to dress this way. It wasn't as if there were lots of female role models I could learn from. Before I knew it, I was sitting before the branch manager, who looked as shocked as all the other brokers who'd just interviewed me. During the interview, he actually shared his belief that women belonged barefoot and pregnant. Seeing that I had nothing to lose, I asked him how much he'd pay me to get pregnant. He said, "Fifteen hundred dollars a month," and to my astonishment he hired me, though he also said that he figured I'd be out of there in six months. To this day, I am convinced I got the job only because he had a women's quota to fill. Before I left the office, I was handed a book on dressing for success. I took the book and went straight to Macy's, opened an account, and charged $3,000 worth of clothes.

I was never so scared in my life as that first day on the job. I knew I didn't belong there. All the stockbrokers drove Mercedeses, BMWs, and Jaguars. I drove a 1967 Volvo station wagon that I bought when I sold the van. They parked their cars in the parking lot; for the first six months, I parked my car on the street because I couldn't afford the lot. I would get tickets knowing that I'd go to court and ask to work the tickets off with community service. The other brokers would eat out at fancy restaurants after the market closed; I got in my car and went to Taco Bell every single day and ate by myself. Still, I felt so lucky and blessed, for even though I was terrified, I was also excited. Every day I was learning new words and concepts—a whole world was opening up to me. It was while studying to take my Series 7 exam, a test all brokers have to pass in order to sell stocks, that I read a rule that stated that a broker needed to know his or her customer— meaning, a broker could not invest a person's money speculatively or risk their money if the customer could not afford to lose it. I had told Randy that I couldn't afford to lose my money, that I was saving up to open a business, that all the money was loaned to me. I realized that Randy had broken this "know your customer" rule.

I marched into the manager's office and told him that he had a crook working for him. He told me that I was a college graduate and I had to know what I was doing when I signed those papers. Besides, he said, that crook made him a lot of money. He told me to sit down, shut my mouth, and keep studying. I went back to my desk. I remembered that when I was hired, the manager had told me I wouldn't last six months. That was just three months away. What did I have to lose? What had happened to me was not right. I had time to make that money back—I was still young—but what if Randy had done this to my mother or my grandmother or any older person? My conscience wouldn't let me keep quiet; I had to do something, for I knew it was better to do what was right than what was easy.

I ended up suing Merrill Lynch—while I worked for them. Now, what I hadn't realized at the time was that because I had sued them, they couldn't fire me. Who knew? Months and months passed as the case proceeded, and during that time I became one of the more successful brokers in the office. Before the lawsuit made it to court, Merrill ended up settling with me. They paid me back all the money plus interest, which allowed me to pay back all the people who had loaned me money.

Whenever I tell this story, people want to know what happened to Fred. When I repaid the money, it surprised me that I didn't hear from him. From time to time I would write or call and leave a message, but I never heard back. Then, in May of 1984, I got the following letter from Fred, who, it turned out, had suffered a stroke—the reason I hadn't heard from him all that time.

Dear Suze,

I had not intended to be this long in writing you a note of appreciation for your check repaying our loan from the Buttercup era. However it seems that words don't come as easily to me as they once did. The check arrived at a critical time in my affairs and for that I am grateful.

That loan may have been one of the best investments that I will ever make. Who else could have invested in a counter girl with porcelain blue eyes and a million-dollar personality and watch that investment mature into a successful career woman who still has porcelain blue eyes and a million-dollar personality? How few investors have that opportunity?

I am working hard to get my affairs in order so that you
and I can both make each other some money. Until then I
would like to remain on your list of friends who wish you
the very best of everything no matter what paths you may
travel in the future.
Fondly,
Fred Hasbrook

Fred passed away a few years ago. I'll never forget the man who
believed in me, who helped me put aside my shame and rewrite
the story history had handed me.

REWRITE THE STORY HISTORY HAS HANDED YOU

I tell you my story not to impress you but to inspire you. I want
you to understand that it is not just our education or what society
has handed us that determines what we can create for ourselves.
It is how you decide to write your own story, how you decide to
live your life.

There are countless examples throughout history and from
various cultures of how women have been disinherited and dis-
enfranchised, so it's no wonder that women today struggle with
their money. It's a foreign experience. Throughout the ages, it was
the man's job to bring money into the family. If you were to lay
out a historical graph that charted women's evolution from non-
earners to earners, our new roles as income producers would
barely rate as a blip. It's that new.

And yet women have come so far so fast in the workplace
since the beginning of the women's movement. Remember the
statistics I cited in the last chapter? Who could have predicted
such rapid, dramatic change in such a short time? At work, we
have overthrown traditions that were centuries—millennia—old.

So why is it that we haven't made the same evolutionary leap when it comes to our personal finances? In my opinion, it has a lot to do with the fact that despite what was going on outside in the world, inside the home traditional roles held tight. Those roles dictated that men handle the finances. Look around—many successful career women today most likely had mothers who abdicated their role in major financial decisions to their husbands, as their grandmothers did and their great-grandmothers before them. The beat of history marches on.

In keeping with my challenge that we use the past to propel us into a new future—that we rewrite the story that history has handed us—I am asking you now to see yourself as an agent of change in your own life and on a global scale. This change is necessary and urgent, given the world we live in today. Consider these realities of our twenty-first-century life:

▲ Social Security is going to replace an even smaller portion of retiree income needs in the decades ahead. What that means is that you are going to have to rely on yourself in retirement much, much more than your parents and grandparents did.

▲ With the divorce rate hovering around 41 percent, many women at some point in their lives will be solely responsible for managing their money. That also holds true for the increasingly large segment of the female population who delay marriage or choose not to marry at all. And, of course, this also includes the growing number of single-parent households.

▲ Even in the marriages that work, money is more of an issue than ever before, especially in homes where there is a stay-at-home mother—making ends meet on one income is a huge challenge these days. I can tell you that the only way to make it work—and I mean the marriage, not the finances—is for both partners to share responsibility for the money decisions. Otherwise, you will be undone by money arguments.

▲ Women on average live about six years longer than men, so it is statistically likely that at some point in your life the family finances will be your concern—and yours alone.

▲ We are also expected to live a lot longer than our parents or grandparents. At the same time, our mothers and fathers are also living longer. That's the good news, but it comes with additional responsibility. Your parents may well need your financial help to maintain their lifestyle as they age or to pay for care they could eventually need.

You get the idea. This isn't your grandmother's world anymore. We are trailblazers.

For the sake of all the mothers who came before you and for the sake of the daughters who will come after you, I'm calling on you to move out of the past and into the future, armed with knowledge and confidence. That means leaving behind old attitudes, old excuses, and tired alibis for not becoming as fully competent and able in the area of personal finance as you are in every other role you inhabit in your life. If you are asked to describe yourself without using the words *mother, grandmother, daughter,* or your job title, I want to hear you say, "I am powerful, I am secure, I am in control of my financial destiny."

No more hiding behind excuses. It's too easy to hide. No shame, no blame. Allowing shame to hold you back—too easy. Blaming others rather than taking responsibility for yourself—too easy. Today I am asking you to do what's right, not what's easy.

You can do this, ladies.

4

YOU ARE NOT ON SALE

Change, I realize, doesn't happen overnight, especially when we are talking about traits and habits that have become embedded in our character thanks to years and years of practice. It is the work of this chapter, then, to call out some particularly damaging forms of self-sabotage, not for the purpose of making you feel bad—remember, there is no shame or blame happening in these pages—but to convince you of the importance of making this attitude adjustment.

The attitude I am referring to is the tendency women have to undervalue themselves. Do you think I'm generalizing? I don't think so. I've got to tell you, I see this trait and its horrible side effects in action so often, it feels like an epidemic to me. So many women—from professionals to stay-at-home moms—treat themselves, their services, and their abilities as if they were always on sale.

I have always said that if you undervalue what you do, the world undervalues who you are. And when you undervalue who you are, the world undervalues what you do. My experience is that women are, unfortunately, masters at both.

NO MORE DISCOUNTING YOURSELF

The big problem as I see it is that women treat themselves as a commodity whose price is set by others. That means women get to stand by and watch as their value is marked down. Tell me if any of the following scenarios sound uncomfortably familiar to you:

▲ Your boss tells you that your raise will be 3 percent this year and yet you know that business is going great, your division is a leader, and you deserve a raise that is at least double what you are getting. You, however, say nothing. You cannot bring yourself to ask for a raise that respects your accomplishments and your worth to the company.

▲ You have a successful business of your own. Your clients love your work, so you get lots of referrals. But even though your operating costs have risen 10 percent in the past three years, you have yet to raise your prices. You are worried you will lose clients if you do. So instead of charging more, you take on a heavier workload to generate more revenue. You work yourself to the bone because you can't seem to value what you do, even though everyone tells you that you do it incredibly well.

▲ You are a stay-at-home mom. Your husband works hard and brings home a decent paycheck. He gives you money each week to run the household, but by the time you've covered all the expenses, there is no money left for you to buy anything for yourself. Since you're not working, you don't feel you have the right to ask him for more. When you really need something, you'll let him know; until then, you're happy to avoid the inevitable tension and humiliation of having your hand out.

▲ You are a massage therapist, a manicurist, a haircutter. You are doing well and making good money. Yet every time a friend or business associate suggests a barter deal in which you swap services "for free," you agree to it. You don't really want to barter—in fact, you don't particularly want the services you will receive in the "trade"—but still you say yes because you are afraid of offending the other person. Bartering doesn't pay the rent or pay down your credit card bill, but for some reason you just can't say no.

▲ You have a full-time job and a full-time family that needs your attention, but when the PTA asks you to help organize the school auction, you sign on. They know they can count on you; every time you are asked to volunteer, you oblige. Volunteering is just what women do, right? It comes with the territory. . . .

Did you find yourself in there somewhere? Do you get it? You treat yourself like you're on sale. You're so reluctant to put a real value on what you do that it diminishes who you are. And as I said, that creates a vicious cycle: When you devalue what you do, it becomes inevitable that you—and those around you—devalue who you are.

When I ask women who run their own businesses why they refuse to raise their prices, they tell me they are afraid to make their needs a priority. When I wonder why a woman who's been a loyal, productive employee doesn't push her boss for a meaningful raise, it becomes clear to me that she's intent on being the good soldier at work. When I see a stay-at-home mom acting as if her husband's paycheck is his and not theirs, I see a woman who does not appreciate the very valuable job of running a household and raising a family.

You need to take yourself off the For Sale rack. Once you learn to respect your right to be fully valued, you will find it easy and natural to ask the world around you to respect that value. You set your price and the world will meet it. When you walk through the world feeling you are "more than" rather than "less than," more will come to you. No one ever achieved financial security by being weak and scared. Confidence is contagious; it will bring more into your life.

It's also important to recognize that your time has value. What I see far too often is that women say yes to giving without calculating the cost of that decision. If you had to put a price to your time, you'd have to take into account the emotional toll and the financial toll of what you are giving away. The financial price is obvious: Are you being compensated fairly for your time? The emotional price is what it takes out of you when you say yes. Too often, both of these measures are overlooked when you are called upon to volunteer, which leads us to . . .

THE VOLUNTEER SYNDROME

It never fails that when I participate in a women's conference or meeting, there is one speaker who makes the point that volunteering is terrifically important for women. It is always the same message: We owe it to society to give back, and we owe it to our children to set a good example of giving back. The audience always nods eagerly in agreement. Now, here is what I find fascinating. I have never once—and I mean not once—heard a male speaker make that point. Men talk about power and success and how money can create more power. Men are comfortable with that. Women are so uncomfortable with the topic of becoming powerful and successful that they have to wrap any discussion of it in the comforting blanket of volunteerism. What is that about? This is not a comment on men; it is simply an observation of what men are told versus what women are told. Again, this is why we have to blast open our past and let it go.

Do men volunteer? Of course. But not in the same way. Men sit on boards, men coach Little League. Women, on the other hand, bake pies, organize the school auction, chaperone field trips. Generally speaking, women tend to take on the more labor- and time-intensive behind-the-scenes tasks. Also, the fact is that more women volunteer than men. A recent national survey reported that 33 percent of women volunteer, compared to 25 percent of men. If it's not encoded in our DNA, then it is certainly the result of the traditional roles of days gone by. Men went off to work; women tended to the home front and created community. Men donated money; women didn't have money of their own to give away, so they gave time. Look at your own life and tell me if this still holds true. My guess is it probably does not, which means that an adjustment of expectations—collectively—is in order.

Now, I want to be very clear here. I am not suggesting that every minute of every day be "on the clock" or that you should never volunteer your time. That is so not my message, I cannot even tell you. Being powerful is not about being selfish, but it does require that you examine your behavior and see where you may be out of balance. And when you do make the decision to donate your time and your effort, know the true worth of what you are giving.

THE BARTERING TRAP

Can you tell me why it is that so many self-employed women find it hard to charge for their services? The minute a friend, business associate, or even a total stranger suggests they "swap" services, they agree. Again, this is not in itself a bad thing to do, but only if you can afford to barter. If you need cash to pay the rent or fund your Roth IRA, then why are you agreeing to swap two hours of your consulting services for one hour of someone else's public relations expertise?

Money is not dirty. Wanting and needing money is not wrong. When you have a healthy relationship with money, you understand its value and importance in building the secure life you seek for yourself and your family. Do not put your time and services on sale—or up for barter—until you are sure you have the money you need to take care of yourself. Money first, barter second. That's the Right Action/Right Relationship.

Now, if you do barter, I want you to make sure that it is a fair swap. If your time is worth $100 an hour, since that is what you charge your paying clients, but your friend who wants to barter does work that is valued at $50 an hour, you are not to do an even-up one-hour swap. You have just devalued yourself again: You are bartering at a rate that is 50 percent below what your time is worth. If you are consciously cutting a deal with your friend because you want to help her out, then that is okay—but again, only if you can really afford to bestow that gift. If you give someone a $50-per-hour break on your work and you give them one hour of your time a week, that is $200 a month you are not making for yourself. If you have high-rate credit card debt, that's $200 you are giving away to someone else rather than getting out of debt. So don't then tell me you can't find the money to invest in a Roth IRA; you just gave away $200. And by the way, if you invested that $200 a month in your Roth IRA every year for the next twenty years, it would grow to more than $118,000, assuming an average 8 percent annual return.

Eye-opening, isn't it? So please be mindful of the cost of bartering. If you can truly afford to barter, great. But please don't make it a default position that you always say yes. Or that you always agree to whatever terms the other party has suggested. When you undervalue what you do, the world undervalues who you are. That's the antithesis of owning the power to control your destiny.

THE VALUE OF DOING WHAT YOU LOVE

There's a category of worker we haven't yet included in this discussion: artists, writers, teachers, activists, and others who have chosen their professions not for the pay but for the satisfaction and nourishment their work brings to their souls. I hope those of you engaged in this type of work realize every day that you are not on sale, that you are doing what you love, and how grateful the rest of us are for what you do.

RAISE YOUR EXPECTATIONS

Given what I do for a living, women are quick to bare their financial lives to me. I love listening, I always try to offer advice when advice is asked for, and in return I am constantly learning how women think and feel about money. Want to know what I see all the time? Women too scared to demand to be paid what they are worth. From stay-at-home moms to executives overseeing multimillion-dollar budgets who get measly raises, to the massage therapist or manicurist afraid to increase her rates, this condition is rampant, and it is a shameful secret women keep, too embarrassed even to tell their closest friends. Luckily, they tend to confess such things to me.

Here's one story: I know a massage therapist who is so fabulous she is very much in demand. Recently, she told me, she was called by a woman who had injured her back. She told the woman that her rate was $80 an hour. The woman thought that was too pricey. "I'll pay you $60 an hour," she told my friend. Do you know what my friend the massage therapist did? She lowered her price to $70 an hour. The woman objected that the price was still too high but agreed, reluctantly, and made an appointment. On the day of the appointment, as my friend was on her way to the woman's house, her cell phone rang. It was the woman—canceling the appointment.

Now, let's look at this. One would tend to blame the woman—how rude that she broke the appointment, how cheap, and so on. But no—the massage therapist brought this on herself. I told her just that. She put herself on sale; when she marked herself down she invited the woman to bargain with her. What if my friend had the power to say, "Listen, actually I'm worth even more than $80, so that's my price, take it or leave it," and the woman had left it? What would have happened? She could have filled that slot with someone willing to pay her full price. She could have saved herself the useless trip out to the woman's house. Or better yet—the woman would have respected her conviction, said fine, and kept the appointment. She'd have loved how she felt afterward and not only made more appointments, but she'd tell everyone she knew how great this massage therapist was.

Listen, I get that people want a bargain. There's nothing wrong with that. But putting yourself on sale is another story. You do that to yourself—no one is doing it to you. You are not a victim of circumstance; in a case like this, you create the circumstance. You can choose to be powerful or powerless. Remember, that choice is always yours.

Here's another story: A friend who works for a major corporation called to tell me she had been approached by a competitor and offered essentially the same job she was doing for her long-time employer, but at nearly double the salary. She was shocked and furious. In that instant, she realized how out of whack her salary was with industry standards and that her employer had been taking advantage of her for years. "This is how you get rewarded for your loyalty," she complained.

My advice to her: Go to her boss and let her know it was time to renegotiate their deal. But first, I told her, she had to let go of her anger and realize that she was complicit in this. She had permitted her employer to take advantage of her all this time. I asked her, "Did you really have no idea that you were making so much less than you should have been making?"

She thought for a moment, then said, "I guess a part of me knew, but I figured we were all in this together. I couldn't imagine that this woman I respected and did good work for would not reward me to the extent she was able. I believed her when she talked about belt tightening."

"And yet you knew your division was making huge profits, right?" I asked.

She realized how naive she sounded. Still, she needed to take responsibility for her role in this. I said, "You go in there and say, 'I realize that I have allowed myself to be unfairly compensated in the past, but now I'd like to correct that and be paid in a way that matches both industry standards and my division's profitability.'"

The lesson here is that you cannot assume that if you simply do good work you will be correctly compensated for your effort. Maybe some of you have truly enlightened bosses who are always quick to give you raises that reflect your effort and your value to the company, but that's not typical. In fact, it's downright rare. This is one area where women can learn from men. Men like to negotiate; men want to negotiate. Rustle some corporate feathers? Hey, a man's gotta do what a man's gotta do.

So many women are made intensely uncomfortable by the thought of having to negotiate their salary. Research shows that women are 2.5 times more likely than men to say they feel "a great deal of apprehension" about negotiating. In one study, men used the metaphor of "winning a ballgame" to describe negotiating, while women picked the metaphor of "going to the dentist." Hmm, a game to be won versus a painful experience . . . The difference in that perspective can cost women a lot. In the book *Women Don't Ask: Negotiation and the Gender Divide,* authors Linda Babcock and Sara Laschever estimate that an unwillingness to negotiate the salary at your first job can end up costing you an estimated $500,000 in lifetime earnings. And it turns out that men are four times as likely to negotiate. In another book, *Get Paid What You're Worth,* two business academics estimate that a woman who actively negotiated her salary over the course of her career could potentially earn $1 million more than if she just settled for what her boss offered. It's pretty clear: If you don't ask, you usually don't get what you deserve.

Here is how to make sure you aren't putting yourself on sale when it comes to your salary:

▲ **Be proactive.** The most important step is to recognize that you need to make this happen. Getting more requires asking for more. If you are not getting what you deserve, you are not to blame your situation on someone else or some external situation. You are responsible for valuing yourself and stating that value to the world. This holds equally true for employees of companies large and small as well as artists and stay-at-home moms.

▲ **Be impatient.** I do not want you sitting around waiting for your boss to magically appear and tell you the company is promoting you and giving you a raise. Take that approach and you could well be waiting a long time. I am not recommending you ask for a raise six months into a job. Be realistic. But if you have gone a long time—say, two years or more—and haven't received a raise, it's time to take action.

▲ **Be prepared.** Tell your boss you want to set up a meeting to discuss your compensation. Prior to that meeting, you are to give your boss a one-page outline of your achievements. Not ten pages, one page. The idea is that you are stating in clear terms what value you have brought to the company and why now is the time for the company to show that it values your effort. The words that should never come out of your mouth are: "I deserve a raise because I haven't had one in two years." If I were your boss, that wouldn't do much for me. But if you state all the ways you have met and exceeded expectations, then you have my attention. The fact that you value what you do causes a nice chain reaction. It gives you the confidence to state your case, and it then makes it difficult for your boss to undervalue your work.

▲ **Those of you who are self-employed of course have a different dynamic to deal with.** You aren't asking a boss for a raise; you are asking your clients for a raise. That seems to send women off the deep end; you would rather sit in an ice bath than discuss new rates with your clients. Do not apologize for raising your rates. Do not sheepishly ask for the increase. You are to tell your clients what your new rate is. You are a businesswoman—emphasis on the business. This is a business decision you are communicating to your clients. They don't have to pay that rate; they can indeed look for other options. But if you are good at what you do and you value your talent, they will not leave. If they do, know that you will be able to find new clients who will pay you what you know you are worth.

Okay, so what if you ask for the raise and your boss looks at you with doleful eyes and says, "I wish I could do more for you, but really, my hands are tied. All I can give you is a standard 3 percent increase this year, because that's the company's policy." Your boss is appealing to your kindness, hoping that you will understand that money is tight, that maybe "next year" will be better. Do you just walk away without gaining anything? Usually you do, right? The female need to be liked, to be seen as a "team player," and your reluctance to speak up for what you deserve cause you to just take whatever your boss says as gospel.

Generosity is a two-way street. If being generous (in spirit, in patience) with your boss isn't being kind to yourself, then you are not acting powerfully. So no matter how uncomfortable your boss tries to make you feel, I want you to stay right in your seat and keep the conversation going. If you know the company is on shaky financial ground, then of course you have to take that into consideration. But if the company is profitable and you are in fact a contributor to that profit, then you are not to walk out empty-handed. Ask that your situation be reviewed in six months and what raise you should expect at that time. Get it in writing that you will have another review/salary discussion in six months—not a year, but six months. In the meantime, if you can't get more salary, negotiate more vacation time. You must get something of value, for you are not on sale.

I have to tell you that if your boss keeps coming back to you with measly raises and new excuses, you need to move on. I know switching jobs is not necessarily easy, nor is it a quick process. But if you work for an employer who does not value what you do, you need to go work for someone who does. When you value yourself enough to reject a bad situation, you are being powerful, and that power will motivate you to find a better job.

THE PURSUIT OF HAPPINESS:
AN E-MAIL FROM MY FRIEND DEBRA

Dear Suze,

Remember when you and I first met a few years ago? You came to address a conference being sponsored by the big Silicon Valley company where I worked. On a break you and I got to talking. I told you that I was considering buying the condo I was renting, and the first question you asked me was whether I was happy in my job. I was so shocked at the question. What did that have to do with me buying a condo? You told me that until I found a job that made me happy, I shouldn't buy anything, because it was the down-payment money I had in my savings account that would give me the freedom to make the move in pursuit of a job that I loved. The answer was so simple, yet it took you asking me about my state of happiness for me to see the light.

You also inspired me to ask for more money the next time I was offered a menial raise from my boss. I had been in my job for nine months when the performance reviews were due just before Christmas. When he called me into his office that week, we spoke for a good twenty minutes (that's a long time for him!) and he expressed how as each day passed, things got better and better and that he was very pleased to have me working for him. Then he presents me with a raise that was the equivalent of mice nuts. I had taken a $3,000 cut in my base pay to work for him, thinking once he saw my work ethic and level of dedication, he would reward it. Well, the joke was on me.

After the holidays, I approached my boss and made him aware that I was glad that he was happy with my performance, but I was quite disappointed in the pay increase. I decided that I wasn't going to back down from asking for more—and didn't—and after three months of going back and forth, he finally gave me the increase I was asking for and made it retroactive! I was so proud of myself for finally standing up for me. It's taken me forever to get to a point where I would do such a thing—my god—I'm going to be 47 in February! But I did it—and it felt really good. So *thank you* for being such an inspiration to me, in my life, in ways that you are completely unaware.

Yours,
Debra

Your goal is that from this day forward you will consciously pay attention to what you need to be paid to feel powerful in your life and secure about your finances. You are to set your value, communicate that value to the outside world, and then not settle for less. Sound daunting? That's just because it takes you out of your comfort zone. You have got to stop being an obstacle on your own path to wealth and security and happiness. You must understand that valuing yourself is well within your control. Do not let others dictate your worth. You are never to put yourself on sale again.

5

THE 8 QUALITIES OF A WEALTHY WOMAN

Now that we've gained some insight into the external forces that tend to make women feel powerless when it comes to matters of money, it is time to learn how to recondition ourselves from the inside. What's required now is that we come from a different place within our beings so that we can realize the potential we all have to become powerful and wealthy. Are you surprised that I used the word "wealthy"? It is still startling for us to hear a woman express a desire to have wealth.

A wealthy women absolutely has money, but she also has happiness, courage, balance, and harmony. A wealthy woman is generous, clean, wise, and therefore beautiful. A wealthy woman has it all, so to speak, and brings these qualities into every relationship, carries them with her in every waking moment of her life.

It's my wish that you will carry these eight qualities within you wherever you go and that they will serve as your guideposts to make sure you are always walking toward wealth rather than walking away from it. It is important that you understand that all eight qualities must be present and work together at all times in order to attain and maintain the true state of a wealthy woman.

Harmony   Balance   Courage   Generosity
Happiness   Wisdom   Cleanliness   Beauty

QUALITIES 1 AND 2: HARMONY AND BALANCE

Harmony is an agreement in feeling, approach, and sympathy. It is the pleasing interaction between what you think, feel, say, and do.

Balance is a state of emotional and rational stability in which you are calm and able to make sound decisions and judgments.

Harmony and balance are perhaps the most important qualities of all, for they serve as the foundation for the remaining qualities. When you possess true inner harmony, what you think, say, feel, and do is one. We are so accustomed to this split-screen state of mind in which we think one thing, say another, feel something else, and act in a way that has nothing to do with what we just thought, said, or felt. When your thoughts, feelings, words, and actions are not in harmony, it shows up as an imbalance—you feel agitated, uncomfortable, you sense something is off, so you find it difficult to make rational, calm decisions. This is why these two qualities are a pair.

To make sure these two qualities are present in your life, you need to pay attention to your feelings. Observe and listen to the words you use—the actions that you take should be perfect reflections of the thoughts you think. If you maintain this awareness, you will notice when you are out of harmony/balance.

When you detect an imbalance, you are to stop whatever it is you are about to say or do and investigate the location of it. Take note when you feel agitated—it's a sign of impairment. If you read the definition of balance again—*a state of emotional and rational stability in which you are calm and able to make sound decisions and judgments*—you will understand that it is an essential cornerstone to a lifetime of correct and powerful behavior.

QUALITY 3: COURAGE

Courage is the ability to face danger, difficulty, uncertainty, or pain without being overcome by fear or being deflected from a chosen course of action.

Courage gives harmony expression. When your thoughts and feelings are one, courage helps you manifest them in the form of words and actions. When you are afraid to speak or act, courage helps you overcome your fear. Courage gives you the ability to speak your truth, even when it is not what others may want to hear.

It can be difficult for women to connect to their courage. Women can be deflected from a course of action if they think that it might hurt someone else. It's so much easier to hurt yourself than to hurt someone else, isn't it? Women also lose their courage when they subscribe to a belief that someone or something is the key to their happiness—rather than recognizing that power lies within.

If you are dependent on your husband or partner to support you, it is easy to lack the courage to speak up on behalf of yourself and your family. Think about it: Are you willing to risk the roof over your head for your needs and wishes?

Fear is usually what stands between us and our courage. We're afraid to rock the boat. We're afraid of confrontation. We're afraid to upset someone. We're afraid we'll lose our job. We're afraid he will divorce us. We're afraid our kids won't love us. We're afraid of what others may think of us. We're afraid we will be flat broke. The list goes on and on. But if we are to embrace this quality of courage to its fullest, we can no longer allow ourselves to hide behind fear.

The only way to conquer fear, finally, is through action. You can meditate on your fear and think about it rationally and try to will it away, but in the end, if fear is preventing you from acting, you must find your courage and act to overcome your fear. You find the courage to silence your fear and you say what's on your mind, you do what you believe must be done, you express your feelings.

And yet, don't think I'm not aware that it's easier said than done.

Suze's Story

There was a time—not that long ago, actually—when it appeared that everything was right in my life. I had three *New York Times* bestsellers, I was on television, I had money, I had fame, and I was doing good, helping people connect to their money and improve their financial lives. I was surrounded by family and a circle of friends and colleagues I was close to . . . and yet something wasn't right. Though in *The Courage to Be Rich* I had written about the need for thoughts, feelings, words, and actions to be one, it took some time for me to locate the source of the imbalance in my own life. I came to see that I had a few friends and professional colleagues who truly did not have my best interests at heart. Though we appeared close on the surface, the truth was we were not. I seemed always to be serving their needs, responding to their schedules, paying attention to what they were doing, while they showed little interest in where my life was taking me—unless it was useful to them in getting ahead in their own careers. If asked, at the time, I would have said I loved them, but in truth, I sure didn't like them, not on any level. And because I had been afraid to speak these thoughts—even to myself—and act upon them, I was robbing myself of my happiness, my power, and my self-respect.

One day, I decided that needed to change. I needed to muster up all of my courage to squelch my fear and to act on what I had been feeling, yet was too afraid to acknowledge, for years now. I took a seriously deep breath and proceeded to do some very dramatic housecleaning. Within a few hours—literally—I ended every one of those relationships once and for all. For the first time in years, I was truly in harmony and balance. I felt proud of myself; despite my fear, I had acted in a way that was true to myself, and the reward was the harmony and balance I was now feeling.

To this day, it remains one of the best things I have ever done. I did an internal housecleaning and made space for other people to come into my life. And when the right people entered my life, it started to soar. I had relationships that were based on truth. I felt the benefits of harmony and balance internally, and I also became more powerful. I had awakened courage that had been dormant, and it started to show up all over the place. The more I used it, the more readily it was there to help me, and my life grew bigger, better, happier, and richer.

QUALITY 4: GENEROSITY

Generosity is when you give the right thing to the right person at the right time—and it benefits both of you.

Generosity is a quality that most women can tap into very easily—maybe too easily, if you ask me. As women, we tend to be overly generous with our time, support, love, and money—but giving simply for the sake of giving does not match the definition of true generosity as stated above.

True generosity goes far beyond what you give to others. In giving there is a power, an understanding that you are just the vessel that wealth or energy flows through. You allow money to come in through your hands and out through your heart. To be empowered to give, to be moved to give straight from the heart, is a feeling that all the money in the world could never buy. That is how I want you to feel when you have been truly generous.

So let me ask you: Is that how you feel when you constantly give of yourself? Do you feel enhanced or do you feel diminished? Be honest here. You think of yourself as a giver, as generous with your time, your talent, your compassion, your money. Others probably describe you as a generous woman, but if I were to look at you, I might think you give for the wrong reasons. Do you give because you feel that you should? Do you give to feel included? Do you give out of guilt or embarrassment? Do you give because you're worried about what others will think if you don't?

It is very important that you understand that *true generosity is as much about the one who gives as it is about the one who receives*. If an act of generosity benefits the receiver but saps the giver, then it is not true generosity in my book.

To me, honest giving must always observe these six rules:

1. **You give to say thank you and out of pure love. Not to get something back.** A true gift has no expectations on it or demands.
2. **Whether it is a gift of time, money, or love, you must feel strongly that your gift is an offering.** It should be given freely and out of pure love.
3. **An act of generosity must never adversely affect the giver.** When you give money that you do not have to give, that gift adversely affects you.
4. **An act of generosity must be made consciously.** You must be aware of how your gift will affect its recipient and make sure it will not be a burden.
5. **An act of generosity must happen at the right time.** You must be able to afford to give your gift, whether it is a material item or the gift of time.
6. **An act of generosity must come from an empathetic heart.** Your generosity should be directed to those who move your heart, those you feel need your help and will treasure the help you give. Giving should enhance you, not diminish you.

QUALITY 5: HAPPINESS

Happiness is a state of well-being and contentment.

When you find the courage to live your life in harmony and balance, when you understand and practice generosity in the truest sense, happiness spontaneously appears.

When you are happy, you are open and accessible. When you are happy, you tend to be more optimistic. You approach new challenges with a clear mind that seeks positive solutions. You see possibilities rather than problems.

If you are not happy, then I would ask you to try to find the place in your life where there is discord and not harmony. Have you wanted to do or say something but failed to find the courage to act? Have you been too giving or generous for the wrong reasons? When you are unhappy, you feel as if something is missing in your life—and that something becomes a hole to be filled. It is dangerous to be in a state of wanting, for it leads to decisions that are not always made with your long-term best interest in mind.

Happiness is not a luxury. It is a necessity for true wealth. When you are happy, you find pure joy in your life. You are not in a state of wanting but a state of contentment. You have the satisfaction of knowing that your actions come from a place of purity and balance, that they are correct and generous and kind. There are no regrets in this state of happiness—and that's a goal worth striving for in all areas of your life.

QUALITY 6: WISDOM

Wisdom is the knowledge and experience needed to make sensible decisions and judgments, or the good sense shown by the decisions and judgments made from an accumulated knowledge of life that has been gained through experience.

The quality of wisdom is more than intellectual, and it is in no way related to how much schooling you have. Exercising wisdom requires cutting through the noise of life and tapping into your core beliefs to make thoughtful decisions. Wisdom results from inhabiting all the qualities that came before it. A wise woman recognizes when her life is out of balance and summons the courage to act to correct it. A wise woman knows the meaning of true generosity. A wise woman knows happiness is the reward for a life lived in harmony, with courage and grace. A wise woman knows how to summon her courage and do what is right, rather than what is easy.

QUALITY 7: CLEANLINESS

Cleanliness is a state of purity, clarity, and precision.

Cleanliness is about respecting the importance of order and organization. When you don't know where your money is, when you have no filing system for your important documents, when you dive into your pocketbook to pull out crumpled bills, when your car looks like a garbage can, when your closets are filled with junk and clutter—I'm sorry, but you cannot possibly be a wealthy woman.

You need to clean up your act—quite literally—to bring true wealth into your life. In India, women sweep the front entrance to their home each morning as a way of welcoming Lakshmi, the goddess of material and spiritual abundance, into their home, for there is a belief that she resides at the threshold of every house. In order for her to enter, she must have a clear path.

Start with your pocketbook and wallet and make sure all bills face the same way and that every morning you put them in order. Next, donate clothing you have not used or worn in the past twelve months to a charity of your choice. Simply throw out all the beauty products that go unused. Remember, when you keep things around you that are worthless to you, they end up making you worthless.

Are your important documents organized? They should be. When your accounts are clean and orderly, you can find the information you need to make good decisions.

▲ **If part of your disorganization is due to document hoarding, on www.suzeorman.com I explain how long you need to hold on to financial records, such as bank statements, mutual fund reports, tax documents, and so on. See page 59 for instructions.**

You might be reading this and thinking that cleanliness is nice but not essential to your financial well-being. I am here to tell you that if this quality is not up front and center and if you do not adhere to it, there is no way you will ever own the power to control your destiny. Wealth will elude you, and you will be left with the mess that you created. Respect the power of this quality of cleanliness. Make it your way of honoring the goddess Lakshmi, if only symbolically. Tell the universe that you have cleared the path for wealth and abundance to enter.

QUALITY 8: BEAUTY

Beauty is the quality or aggregate of qualities in a person that gives pleasure to the senses or pleasurably exalts the mind or spirit.

Beauty is what you create when you incorporate the other seven qualities into your life. When you take the steps to have harmony, balance, courage, generosity, happiness, wisdom, cleanliness, and beauty in your life, you will exude confidence in who you are. And there is nothing more beautiful than a confident woman. Remember, when you are confident you feel secure, and when you feel secure you have no fear. And when you have no fear, you have the courage to say what you think and feel in a calm and wise way. And when you are calm, you make wise decisions with your money, which then allows you to be truly generous to others as well as yourself, which, in turn, makes you a happy, powerful, and beautiful woman. Do you see how all of these qualities work together to help you arrive at the goal of being a woman in control of her destiny?

SUMMONING THE 8 QUALITIES

I've noticed, in my own life and in others', that the more you summon these qualities, the easier they are to access. Harmony yearns for more harmony, and balance abhors imbalance. Courage begets greater courage. Once you are generous in the right way, a lesser form of generosity will feel inferior to you. True happiness will never permit you to settle for a lesser form of happiness. Cleanliness recoils at disorder. Wisdom, once achieved, is with you forever, and beauty inspires beauty in all things.

Carry these qualities with you throughout your life. Write them on a notecard and keep them close at hand—in your wallet or in your pocket. Make it into a talisman to guide you every day as you make your way through life and all its impossible demands. These qualities will keep you focused and tranquil. Let them and they will offer you constant reassurance that you are acting powerfully and correctly, with love in your heart and the purest intentions, to realize your goals of security and comfort for yourself and all you love.

Harmony   Balance   Courage   Generosity
Happiness   Wisdom   Cleanliness   Beauty

6

THE SAVE YOURSELF PLAN

When it comes to money and why we haven't done what we know we should, we can endlessly debate *why this* and *why that* until we are all blue in the face. We can make sure that you are thinking the right thoughts and saying the right words, but at the end of the day you have to stop talking and just start doing. Are you still afraid? If you are, that's okay, but there is only one way to conquer fear, and that is through action. That's why I have devised The Save Yourself Plan.

The Save Yourself Plan includes a combination of actions to take as well as concepts and principles to learn. The learning part of the plan is crucial for your long-term success. It will equip you with the knowledge you need to act correctly and confidently whenever life presents you with a new financial challenge or choice.

I am not going to ask you to devote hours on end to some exhaustive quest for financial knowledge. The Save Yourself Plan focuses solely on the core foundations of personal finance that you *must* know and take care of. What I am going to ask you to do and to learn is a pared-down version of advice I have written about in great detail in my previous books. I know that many of you have read those books from cover to cover. The fact that you are reading this book, however, tells me that, for whatever reason, you weren't able to act on what you read.

That's where The Save Yourself Plan comes in. It is written with the assumption that we should begin with the basics and not take anything for granted. Basic definitions and explanations are exactly what you will find here: The Save Yourself Plan assumes no prior financial vocabulary or knowledge. We start at the very beginning and we will move forward—together—from there.

The plan is all about simplicity. While I was creating it, I constantly reminded myself to focus on this one clear goal: "If all you did was X, I would be thrilled." The challenge for me was to make sure that X is everything you need to know and do, but nothing more than what is absolutely essential and achievable. It's sort of like the world of cookbooks. Some cookbooks are a great read, and you ogle the fabulous photos, but the recipes are way too involved, the ingredients too hard to find, and the techniques far too complex for you ever to attempt to actually make any of the dishes. Those books are for the coffee table, not the kitchen. Then there are the other kind of cookbooks, the kind that stay close to the stove. They have the recipes you can easily pull off in a reasonable amount of time. That's what I had in mind when I created The Save Yourself Plan: core financial recipes that are easy to follow and simple to create.

The plan is divided into five distinct sections, with an expectation that you will tackle one section a month. We will spend the first two months taking control of spending and basic savings, handling your bank accounts and credit cards, and mastering your FICO credit score. Month Three is all about retirement investing, including what to do through work and what you need to do on your own. Then we will face up to the critical documents every woman needs to have in place in Month Four. Month Five is all about protection: what you need in life insurance and home insurance to make sure you and your family will be financially secure no matter what life brings. Finally, I will let you know what I expect of you beyond the plan. It's an integrative approach that seeks to make what was once alien to your life a natural part of it—for the rest of your life.

> Given the plan's minimalist approach, I anticipate there will be moments where some of you may wish I had gone into more detail or had discussed a financial topic that isn't addressed in these pages. That's why I have built a special **Save Yourself** destination on my website. When you see ▲ in the book, you will find information on related topics that are covered at **www.suzeorman.com**. To gain access to the **Save Yourself** information, you will have to register by entering your name, your e-mail address, and the special access code: **EIEIO**. I urge you to visit this online resource and have a look around. You'll find a vast and very useful array of advice, tools, and forms—and they're all free to readers of *Women & Money*. You'll also learn why I've chosen this icon ▲ as the symbol for **Save Yourself**.

At the start of each month, you will see the "I Would Be Thrilled" box, which provides a quick overview of the financial moves you will master that month. And at the end of each month you will find the "Action Plan" box, which is a To Do list of the powerful moves I want you to make that month.

All I ask is that you give me a maximum of one full day's time in each month—twenty-four hours total—to complete the tasks

I have laid out for that month. One way to look at it is that the time spent will be the equivalent of just five days over five months. It is completely up to you how you schedule the work; it can be a series of hour-long mini-sessions spread throughout the month, or you may choose to designate the better part of a few days each month to the tasks at hand.

The five-month time frame is simply a rational target I am confident every woman can hit. Given that I am asking for a total of about five days' worth of "active" time, I imagine some of you will want to complete The Save Yourself Plan in just a month or two. That's fine. But don't pressure yourself into rushing through everything. There are no gold stars for speed. What you will learn—and do—from the plan is the financial foundation for the rest of your life; take your time to complete the work at a pace that is comfortable for you and that ensures that you truly understand everything you are doing.

It is very important for you to work your way through the plan in the order in which I present the information. In other words, I want you to read through and follow the action steps in Month One, before launching into Month Two. And there is a logical progression built within each month, so please don't skip around. Everything is in its place for a reason.

For the best results, I also ask that you not fly past sections you think you don't need to read because you have already taken care of that topic in your own life. Or because you have let someone else—a husband, partner, brother, uncle, financial advisor—take care of it for you, and they assure you everything is "in place." I don't care if Warren Buffett is your financial advisor. Power doesn't come from relying on someone else to handle your money. It is created when you—and only you—take the initiative to learn about your money and to make sure that you have what you need. That's my definition of power. And it's as much about reviewing what you already have as it is about taking new steps to build security. For example, even if you have a savings account, I still want you to read through what I have to say so that you can make sure you have the best savings account available. And if you have life insurance, don't flip past the life insurance section. I can't tell you how many women assure me they have life insurance. But, once I extract some details, they are shocked to learn they don't have the correct type of life insurance and don't have enough coverage to truly protect themselves and their loved ones.

In some instances, I will recommend you do something solely for yourself, such as setting up a savings account that is in your name only. In other instances, you will need to review joint investments and financial documents with your husband or partner or whomever you have entrusted your financial life to. Make it clear to them that you are not challenging or questioning their choices. This is not about them. It is all about you and your desire to become powerful through understanding whether what you have is indeed what you—and they—need. In the chapter after The Save Yourself Plan, we cover how to create new, healthier financial relationships with those you love. That includes advice on how to navigate taking a more active role in the family finances your spouse or partner has been solely responsible for over the years.

Controlling your financial destiny, forever shedding a lifetime of money fear, shame, and confusion, is just five months away.

Month One:
Checking and
Savings Accounts

I WOULD BE THRILLED IF YOU . . .

... Learned to read your bank statement and balance your checkbook.

... Stopped paying for basic checking services.

... Understood the difference between a checking account and a savings account.

... Appreciated that a savings account is the cornerstone of financial security.

... Made sure the interest rate you earn on your savings account is as high as possible.

... Used a monthly automatic investment plan to build up a savings account that can cover up to eight months of living expenses.

... Opened a savings account just for yourself, in addition to any family savings account.

A home builder will tell you a house is only as good as the foundation it rests on. The same is true with your finances. And that means starting off by making sure you have control of your basic checking and savings accounts. Emphasis on "control." I bet every one of you has both a checking and a savings account, but that doesn't mean you really understand how they work, or whether you have the best deal going, or that you understand how to manage both so that you know—not guess, but *know*— that you can pay the bills this month and have enough money put away to cover any unexpected financial emergencies.

So this month is all about banking. We'll first learn the ins and outs of checking accounts, then move on to savings accounts.

DEFINITIONS YOU NEED TO KNOW

- ▲ A **savings and loan** is pretty much exactly like a bank; the differences have more to do with the fact that a bank offers commercial loans to businesses, whereas S&Ls don't.
- ▲ A **credit union** is a financial institution that offers the same services as a traditional bank; the big difference is that it is a nonprofit supported by its members—that is, the people who have accounts at the credit union. Each credit union has its own membership rules; for instance, a credit union may be just for schoolteachers in a particular district or school system, or members of the military, or professionals in the same field of practice. Quite often you can become a member of a credit union simply if you know someone who qualifies.
- ▲ A **brokerage firm** is a financial institution where you can purchase a range of investments (stocks, bonds, ETFs, mutual funds, and so forth) and deposit money into various types of savings accounts, such as money market accounts.

In the following pages, when I refer to banks, I also mean accounts you can have at brokerage firms, savings and loans, and credit unions.

If you currently use a credit union or S&L, that's fine, as long as you are getting all the services I describe below. The most important feature, no matter what specific type of institution you use, is that it insures your deposits. You want to know that no matter what happens to that institution your money is safe and sound, and that is accomplished with insurance. At most financial institutions, the insurance comes from the Federal Deposit Insurance Corp. (FDIC). If you use a credit union, you must make sure it offers insurance from the National Credit Union Administration or a state insurance plan.

CHECKING ACCOUNTS

Your checking account should be for one purpose and one purpose only: cash you need to pay your bills and have handy in your wallet. That's it. It is not where you keep last year's bonus or money you are saving for a home down payment or spa vacation. It is all about your day-to-day cash flow. The big problem is that so many of you take the dread/prayer approach to cash-flow management. You dread the monthly ritual of looking at your checking account statement and pray you have enough cash in the bank to cover the bills. Where's the control in that?

Your first step this month is to take responsibility for balancing your checkbook and to keep at it every month from now on. I know that doesn't sound terribly exciting, but it is probably the most empowering move you will ever take toward controlling your destiny. **The process of balancing your checkbook forces you to deal with reality.** When you sit down and stare at your deposits for the month compared to your withdrawals for the month, you push yourself into a position of responsibility for your spending.

If you already balance your checkbook every month and have control over the flow of money coming in and going out, then you can jump down to the section on savings accounts. Everyone else, keep reading.

Start Fresh—Open Up a New Checking Account

I recommend starting with a completely new checking account so from day one you know exactly what you have, rather than trying to make sense of an old checking account to which you have never paid much attention. So after you pay your bills this month, I want you to stop using your current checking account. Leave it open and leave in the account whatever money is needed to cover the checks you have already written on that account until every check has been cashed by the person or company you paid. Also, do not use your ATM card on that old account again. Now I want you to take whatever money is not needed to cover those outstanding checks and new money that you will be getting in your next paycheck and immediately open up a brand-new checking account and get a new ATM card.

It is perfectly fine to open your new account at your current bank, as long as it is a good deal. By that I mean you aren't nickeled and dimed to death with all sorts of fees. Remember, just because you had a checking account at a bank does not mean it was a good checking account. Here is what constitutes a good checking account.

A Good Checking Account Has

▲ No monthly fee for simply having the account.
▲ A low required balance to qualify for free checking (no monthly fee).
▲ Free checks and check writing.
▲ Online access to your account statements and free online bill pay.
▲ Insurance coverage of your deposits.

Don't Pay Monthly Fees

There's really no excuse for paying a monthly fee for your checking account. There are plenty of banks eager enough for your business that they will give you a checking account with no monthly fee and without requiring you to keep a four-digit balance. Below I will explain where to find the fees on your statement so you know what you have been paying in the past.

The Only Type of Checking Account You Want

There are two basic types of checking accounts: interest-bearing and non-interest-bearing. Interest is the money the bank pays you for the money you keep in the account (your balance). I know it would seem to make sense that getting paid interest on your checking account is the smart way to go, but it rarely is. Here's what you need to understand: The actual interest rate you are paid on checking accounts tends to be really low compared to the interest rate you can earn on other types of bank accounts. And to avoid monthly fees on an interest-bearing account, you are often required to keep a high balance—$2,500 or more. That doesn't really make sense, because you aren't being paid a good interest rate on the balance they require you to keep in the account.

For example, at the start of 2007 it was typical for an interest-bearing checking account with a $2,500 balance to pay less than 1 percent interest, which works out to less than $25 a year in interest credited to your account. But if your balance dips below the required minimum balance—and $2,500 is a typical cutoff—you will be hit with a monthly fee of $10. Do that three times a year and you end up paying more in fees ($30) than what you earn in interest. Besides, it's better to keep your checking account balance as low as possible to cover your bills and cash needs, and put all your "extra" money in a savings account—but more on this later. In January 2007, you could find a savings account that pays you about 5 percent. That's a lot better than what you can typically get on your checking account.

Shop for a Better Checking Account

If your current bank doesn't offer any fee-free checking accounts, I recommend you get on the Internet and go to www.bankrate. com and click on the "Checking and Savings" tab on the top of the page. Once you are in that section, you can search for the best bank deals in your area by clicking on the "Compare Rates" link in the box on the right side of the page.

Pay Bills Online

I also recommend signing up for online bill payment—a service that should be free. With online bill payment you don't need to write out checks and send them through the mail; instead, you can set up automatic electronic payments directly from your checking account. Worried about the safety of using a computer to handle your banking? Don't be. Banks spend a lot of money and effort making sure their networks are secure—that is, that identity thieves can't get at your information. In fact, paying your bills online may actually be safer than mailing them in.

Update Your Automatic Deposits and Withdrawals

Once you set up your new checking account, be sure to update all your automatic deposits and withdrawals that you may have already had in place with your old account. If your paycheck is directly deposited into your checking account, notify your human resources department that you now want your paycheck sent to your new checking account. If you also have set up direct payment from your checking account to pay ongoing bills, you'll need to notify those companies of your new account information.

ATM Visits

Okay, now we're ready for a fresh start to cash-flow management. The simple goal is to keep track of what's coming in and what's going out. That begins with documenting your ATM withdrawals. Every time you use the ATM I want you to get a printed record of the transaction, put it in a special section of your wallet, and then once a week empty that part of the wallet into a special folder you have just for bills and ATM slips. And I mean a real folder, or manila envelope, or a cardboard box—your choice. My only stipulation is that it be a storage option solely dedicated to your ATM and banking records. The kitchen drawer that is also home to the school call list, the takeout menus, and Ziploc bags is not allowed. Taking control requires knowing where your documents are and being able to pull them out in seconds.

Open and Organize the Bills

I also want you to create another dedicated storage place for all the bills you receive by mail. It can be another folder, a basket, or a special drawer in your office desk. Again, the only requirement is that the space be dedicated for this one task: storing the bills you need to pay for that month. Every day you are to separate your mail; the bills are to be instantly whisked off to your special storage file/folder/box. Control = Organization.

Before you toss the bill in your storage spot, I am asking that you first open every piece of financial mail and give it a quick scan—just to make sure nothing is out of line and to note the due date. This simple process of opening and scanning your bills and statements as they come in is how you start to build a healthy relationship with your money. Nothing gets lost, nothing gets overlooked, and there are no surprises the day before your payments are due. You are on top of it all, with very little effort: The process of sorting the mail and opening the bills takes only an extra few minutes a day.

Ideally, you want to sit down and pay all your bills once a month; it's a great way to stay organized. If you currently have multiple credit card bills with due dates all over the month, call up customer service and ask to have your due date moved. Card issuers aren't required to do this, but many will. If the card company won't budge, or you have to spread your payments out over the course of the month to coincide with your paycheck deposits, that's okay. The point is that you want to make it a systematic ritual that you commit to so you can stay organized. If that needs to be every two weeks, that's fine. The important thing is that you stop paying bills on the fly without keeping track.

When you are ready to pay your bills and balance your checkbook, sit down at your computer and sign on to your bank's website so you can view your current bank statement. Please don't use a public computer to do this, and if you have a wireless laptop, I would refrain from doing your balancing act at the coffee shop. It just makes the most sense to access your account from home, where you can be assured your Internet connection is protected by a security firewall.

Basically, what we are going to do is look at all the money you have taken out of your account that month (what shows up under the "Debits" column on your statement) and all the money that you have deposited into your account during the month (what shows up under the "Credits" column on your statement).

Checking for Fees That You Should Not Be Paying

I want to start by first assessing your laziness factor. I am talking about all the extra fees you get hit with if you aren't on top of your account. These will show up in your statement either as fees or debits. This is what you should look for:

▲ **ATM fees.** Your own bank should not charge a penny to use its ATMs; if it does, you need a new bank. But we all know that when we use an ATM from another bank we will get hit with a fee; actually, it is typically two fees: one charged by the bank whose ATM you used, and one by your bank for dealing with the outside bank. If you get hit on both ends, that can easily cost you $3 per transaction.

▲ **Bounced-check fees.** Write a check that you can't cover and you get smacked with a charge of $25 or so. Even worse is the "overdraft" coverage banks love to offer: The bank will cover your overdraft—assuming it isn't more than, say, $1,000—and charge you $35 for the service, plus a daily charge of $2 to $10 until you deposit enough money in the account to cover the overdraft amount.

Now, what did all those fees you paid last month add up to? Or the month before? Be honest with yourself; are you constantly getting hit with a fee here and there that you simply shrug off? You have to understand that power starts with appreciating that no fee is too small to ignore. Let's say you run up $6 a month in ATM fees and over the course of the year you bounce three checks. That's about $150 in fees each year ($72 for the ATM fees and about $75 or so for the bounced checks). That's $150 you didn't have to pay; only your laziness is to blame. And don't you dare tell me it is "only" $150. If instead of blowing $150 a year for ten years you invested it in a savings account that paid a 5 percent interest rate, you would have nearly $2,000 saved up. That's what your laziness is costing you.

Verify All Deposits and Withdrawals

Next, I want you to pull out your ATM folder for the month. While it is extremely rare for banks to make mistakes, that doesn't mean mistakes don't ever happen. So verify that every deposit and withdrawal you made at an ATM shows up on the statement.

And take a minute to add up the total of all your ATM withdrawals for the month. This is typically a shocker the first time you do it. My experience is that we all tend to forget at least one or two withdrawals each month.

> ▲ **If you can't fathom where all the money went, I recommend keeping a log of your cash spending for a few months. Once you see some clear spending patterns, it becomes easier to strategize how you can scale back your spending so you have more left over at the end of the month. On my website is a worksheet for tracking your cash.**

Now pull out your pay stubs for the month and make sure that all your direct deposits were in fact credited to your account. Again, mistakes are rare, but you never know.

Now you're ready to pay the bills. As I explained earlier, if possible this should be a once-a-month ritual. It's hard to keep track of your money when you are constantly writing checks throughout the month. Whether you use online bill payment or do it the old-fashioned way, it is pretty simple: You are to make sure that every check you write is documented as a Debit on your account, and you subtract all your Debits from your balance (Credits). Obviously, the goal is that you have more than enough in your Credit column to cover all your Debits—that is, once you finish writing all the checks, you have a positive bank balance.

Don't Fall for Check Bouncing and Overdraft Coverage

Please do not rely on your bank's promise of "free" or "courtesy" check-bouncing coverage. As I already explained, it's anything but free. I also don't want you to rely on signing up for a system where if your checking account hits zero, your bank is authorized to tap into your savings account or a credit card to come up with the cash to cover your bills. Sure that's convenient, but once again, you really aren't taking control of the situation—you are just reducing your own savings or adding to your credit card debt to deal with your cash-flow problem. It's your own personal version of robbing Peter to pay Paul.

The far better long-term game plan is to take a hard look at your spending and see where you can trim back so you aren't on the verge of overdrawing your account every month.

> **If you are having trouble meeting your bills each month, I have tips for how to reel in your spending so you have more left over at the end of each month to cover your bills.**

SAVINGS ACCOUNTS

Now that we have an understanding of what to look for in a checking account and how to use it, the other pillar of financial security is a savings account, where you have no risk of losing a penny and the bank will pay you for keeping your money on deposit.

There are various types of savings vehicles and they go by different names, depending on whether you open a savings account at a bank, a mutual fund company, or at a brokerage firm. For example, a money market deposit account (MMDA), which is also commonly referred to as a money market account (MMA), that is opened with a brokerage firm is basically an account within an account—meaning that you open a brokerage account and within it is a place to hold and save your money. The brokerage account that houses the money market account provides you with more options than just saving; it allows you to buy various investments, be they stocks, bonds, mutual funds, CDs, or even gold. A simple savings account opened at a bank typically doesn't afford you any of these other investment options.

For the purposes of this chapter, I am using the term money market account to include money market deposit accounts, since they are essentially the same thing.

Know the Difference Between Checking and Savings Accounts

I want to be very clear about one thing: A checking account is not a savings account, and a savings account is not a checking account. I want you to have both types of accounts, but it is crucial that you understand they have different uses. As we just saw, your checking account is where you keep money you need to cover your monthly spending. Whether it be cash you take out at the ATM, or checks you write to cover bills, your checking account is where that money comes from. It is the ultimate in banking convenience; you can withdraw money at any time—be it by check or ATM—though the trade-off for that convenience is that you rarely can find a checking account that also pays you a good interest rate on your balance.

A savings account can be a bit less convenient than a checking account—there can be some restrictions on the number of withdrawals you can make or a minimum withdrawal amount, for example—but the bank will pay you a higher rate of interest on your money than it does on its typical checking accounts. Those small restrictions should not be a problem, because your savings account isn't for your day-to-day spending; you've got that covered with your checking account.

How a Savings Account Will Help You Save Yourself

A savings account is where you build up a sum of money so when a big unexpected bill arrives, you have the security of knowing you can handle it without having to borrow money or fall back on your credit card (or bounce a check on your checking account). A savings account is where you get the $700 to pay the mechanic after your car conks out. It is where you come up with the $1,000 to cover your health insurance deductible when your child needs some special tests that aren't covered by your plan. Your emergency cash fund is also the safety net that keeps you from panicking if you are unexpectedly laid off, because you know you have enough in your savings account to cover your basic living costs until you get a new job. And a savings account is what makes it possible for you to move out of a bad relationship and into your own place. If you keep "emergency money" in your checking account, you are making a costly mistake. You can earn a lot more interest by keeping your emergency fund in a savings account.

Understand How Interest Works

When I refer to earning money on your account, I am talking about what the financial institution pays you for keeping your money on deposit with them. That payment is calculated as a percentage rate. The percentage rate goes by a few different names: interest rate, yield, and annual percentage yield (APY) are the most common. They are all slightly different versions of the same essential concept: how much money you will make on the money you keep deposited in your account. Keeping to my promise of simplicity, I am not going to insist that you learn the nuances of every term. Instead, I want you to focus on just one: annual percentage yield (APY). Whenever you look at an ad or get a sales pitch for a savings account, you want to focus on the annual percentage yield. This is the best measure of what you will really earn. If you are comparing different accounts at different financial institutions, always ask for the APY so you will be comparing apples to apples.

Get the Highest APY

As I mentioned, most "interest-bearing" checking accounts pay a small rate of return—less than 1 percent typically. What you get in convenience you give up in earning power. By comparison, some online savings accounts had an APY of about 5 percent as of the start of 2007.

I know percentages can be a bit numbing, so let's convert all of this to dollars. If you have a checking account with a balance of $2,000 and the APY is 1 percent, you will be paid a total of $20 over the course of the year in interest. Now let's say that instead you kept that $2,000 in a savings account and you earned the 5 percent APY. That comes to $100 in interest. Big difference, right?

Bottom line: Your checking account should have only the money you need to cover your monthly bills and cash outlays. Money you want to have for emergencies belongs in a savings account where you can earn money. Power comes not just from saving money, but from saving your money in an account that pays you the most you can get.

A Savings Account of Your Own

Every woman should have her own savings account that is completely separate from any other savings account shared with a spouse, partner, parent, child, et cetera. There is no need to hide this account from anyone. There is nothing shameful or suspicious in establishing your own savings. It goes back to what we discussed in the earlier chapters of this book: Taking care of yourself is not secondary to everything else and everyone else. You deserve to have financial security that is all yours, that you know you can always rely on in a personal emergency.

I believe in this principle so passionately that I have news of an incredibly special offer for the readers of this book— one that puts into action all these words and provides an unprecedented incentive that is nearly impossible to refuse. See the box on page 85 for details.

What You Need to Save

A savings account that serves as an emergency cash fund should be large enough to cover at least eight months of living expenses; this applies to both couples and single women. I am being very careful here to protect you from major financial setbacks. For example, the more advanced your career, the longer it can take to find a job comparable in salary to the one you left. A big savings account is also protection against unexpected medical bills; the sad truth is that one of the major reasons for personal bankruptcies in the United States is unpaid medical bills.

As I mentioned, those of you in a relationship need an additional savings account that is just in your name. Your separate account should have enough money in it to cover at least three months of living expenses. I never want any woman to stay in a relationship because she feels financially trapped; that savings account of your own is your freedom account. I hope you never need to use it, but power is knowing you have it just in case.

So if it costs you $3,000 a month to live and you are single, you need to have at least $24,000 in a savings account as an emergency fund. If you are in a relationship, your family account would be $24,000, and your personal account would be $9,000.

With respect to how to juggle funding both accounts I would do this by equally dividing what you have to save 50/50. So if you have $200 to save every month, $100 goes into your own emergency fund, and $100 goes into the family fund. I know that might sound selfish, but it is important to know you have money that is just your own. It does not mean that you do not love your family; it is just something that you need to do for yourself. And every couple needs to create a system for having separate money. In the chapter entitled "The Commitments," I will explain why couples also need to make sure that after meeting all their joint financial obligations they split any extra money left at the end of the month and give each other the freedom to spend or save their share as they please. My recommendation is that women— especially stay-at-home moms—use their share of the extra money left at the end of each month to build their own emergency cash fund. This is not about trust; this is about what is needed for you to feel truly independent—truly powerful in your life.

Now, I realize that many of you may not even have eight weeks saved up, let alone eight months. Don't be discouraged. The key is to commit to starting to save as much as you can each month. It may take you a year, or three years, or more to reach your goal. As long as you do your best to put money away consistently, you are acting powerfully.

Save on Autopilot

The best way to build a savings account is to set up a system where you authorize the bank where you have your checking account to automatically transfer money each month from that account into a savings or money market account. It doesn't have to be at the same bank. Using an auto-transfer system takes it out of your hands, and let's face it, that's probably a very smart move. You don't have to remember to put money in your savings account, and you are not able to give yourself a free pass one month when you feel like spending rather than saving. By setting up an automatic electronic monthly transfer, you are forcing yourself to save.

You can choose the auto-deposit option when you sign up for a savings account. If you already have an account, contact customer support and ask how to establish this service. It is very simple to put into place. You typically need to provide the institution where you have your savings account two pieces of information: the account number on your checking account and the "routing number" for the bank where you have your checking account. Your bank's routing number is the first nine numbers on the lower left portion of your check. Or just call up your bank and ask for the routing number. With those two pieces of information, both institutions will be able to talk to each other and get this automatic recurring transfer set up for you.

Whatever you can afford to put away each month is the right amount for you. Only you can know for sure how much you can afford to save. All I ask is that you respect yourself: Don't let yourself off with the excuse that you can't afford to save anything. It may take some sacrifice, but if you want to gain financial security by building a large savings account, you must be willing to take a serious look at your spending and see where you might find areas to scale back so you have money for your savings account.

For tips on how to find more money for savings, go to my website.

And don't think it has to be a lot of money each month.

If you put this much in your savings account each month ...	and your account has an APY of 5%, you will have this much saved up:			
	In one year	*In three years*	*In five years*	*In ten years*
$50	$614	$1,938	$3,400	$7,764
$100	$1,228	$3,875	$6,801	$15,528
$200	$2,456	$7,751	$13,601	$31,056

On my website I have a calculator where you can input your expected monthly savings and the APY you can currently earn, to estimate how your savings account will grow over time.

How to Size Up a Savings/Money Market Account

A good savings/money market account charges no fees and the APY you earn is as high as possible. The trick is knowing what's a good rate.

Follow the Fed

The APY on a savings/money market account is not set in stone. In financial terms, the rate floats rather than being fixed (permanent). A financial institution can offer any rate, and the rates can vary widely from bank to bank. But all banks tend to follow the lead set by the Federal Reserve. The Federal Reserve is our government's big bank. It has all sorts of power and sets all sorts of policy, but the one and only thing you should know is that the head honchos at the Fed meet eight times a year and decide if they want to raise, lower, or leave unchanged a key interest rate known as the Federal Funds Rate. Banks follow the Federal Reserve's lead: When the Federal Funds Rate rises, you typically see interest rates on savings/money market accounts rise. When the Federal Funds Rate falls, so too will the rates. Some financial institutions react instantly; others may make the adjustments monthly or quarterly. The point is that if you know what the Fed Funds Rate is—it's always news when the Fed announces its moves and is easy to find in the business section of most newspapers or online—you know a good savings rate should be right around that rate.

For example, at the end of 2006, the Federal Funds Rate was 5.25 percent. So a good savings rate should be between 4.5 and 5 percent. At the same time, though, plenty of places offered savings accounts with APYs of just 2 percent or 3 percent. Sticking with a low-paying savings account is crazy. If your account is more than three-quarters a percentage point (0.75) below the Federal Funds Rate, I think you should move your money to an account with a higher yield.

One important caveat: I realize that some of you may have a good no-fee deal at your current bank because your combined balances on your checking and savings accounts are large enough. So if you pull out your savings, you may no longer qualify for the free checking. If that's the case, be proactive and move your checking account at the same time you move your savings account. As I mentioned, www.bankrate.com is a great place to shop for no-fee checking accounts. You can also search for top savings accounts.

Opening a new account can take you as little as ten minutes. As of late 2006, some of the banks offering the highest APYs are Internet banks. Here are a few of my favorites:

▲ Emigrant-Direct: www.emigrant-direct.com
▲ HSBC: www.hsbcdirect.com
▲ ING Direct: www.ingdirect.com

Beyond Savings Accounts

A savings or money market account is all I insist you have, but I also want you to know that there are other good savings options, such as certificates of deposit (CDs) and money market mutual funds (MMMFs), both of which are available at banks, mutual fund companies, and brokerage firms.

 If you are interested in learning about CDs and MMMFs, and when it makes to sense to add them to your savings strategy, go to my website.

A Word on Safety

Online banks, "bricks-and-mortar" banks—including savings and loans—and brokerage firms can all be part of the Federal Deposit Insurance Corp. (FDIC) program. The first thing you should check when looking into a financial institution where you want to keep your money safe is whether it is an FDIC member. Most banks are, and they love to let you know about it: You typically will see "FDIC" on the website homepage, or plastered on the bank's front door and just about everywhere else they can think of. Credit unions have a similar insurance system. Look for a sign stating that your credit union is a member of the National Credit Union Share Insurance Fund (NCUSIF) or is covered by a state-operated insurance plan.

The FDIC is a federal agency that protects depositors (that's you) at its member banks, brokerages, and S&Ls. If the institution runs into trouble and can't pay you the money you have on deposit, the FDIC steps in and covers your deposits up to certain limits.

These rules apply at places that offer insurance:

▲ *$100,000 for individual accounts*
Up to $100,000 of your combined deposits in checking and savings accounts is fully insured. This insurance is per institution. So if you have $100,000 at one institution and $100,000 at another, your combined $200,000 is fully insured. Please note: They must be entirely different institutions, or credit unions, not different branches of the same institution.

▲ *$200,000 for jointly held accounts*
In addition to your individual coverage, you can also have a combined $200,000 in an account you own with someone else, such as a spouse or partner. That $200,000 breaks down into $100,000 of insurance for each of you.

▲ *$100,000 per each account with a designated beneficiary*

You can also receive $100,000 of insurance for every account that you will give to someone else upon your death. That is, you sign an agreement that upon your death the money goes to the person listed on the account as your beneficiary. For example, if you have four grandchildren and set up four separate bank accounts at the same institution of $100,000 each, with each grandchild as the beneficiary of an account, all $400,000 is insured. Or you can set up one account for $400,000 and name each of the four grandchildren as beneficiaries, with each child receiving $100,000 of insurance coverage.

▲ *$250,000 for IRA accounts*

If you have an IRA account at an insured bank or credit union, those retirement assets are covered for up to $250,000. (Again, this is per bank/credit union.) But please be very careful with this. The IRA insurance is only for certain types of accounts you can buy through a bank, credit union, or brokerage firm, such as money market deposit accounts (MMDAs) and certificates of deposit (CDs). It does not cover any stocks or stock mutual funds that you may have purchased through them.

What's Not Covered by FDIC Insurance

Banking was a whole lot easier years ago when the only accounts offered were simple savings and checking accounts and CDs. But banks—and S&Ls and credit unions—are now able to offer all sorts of other types of investments, such as mutual funds. And you can even buy stocks through a bank subsidiary. In Month Three of The Save Yourself Plan I explain in detail what mutual funds and stocks are and how they work, but the important thing to understand right now is that mutual funds and stocks can lose value; that is, if you invest $1,000 in a mutual fund or a stock, you are not guaranteed that you will always have at least $1,000 in the account. If the stock market goes up, you will have more than $1,000. If the stock market goes down, you will have less than $1,000. That's why they are called investments and not deposits. That's a crucial difference. Deposits are insured. Investments aren't. Even if you bought them at a bank and you get a statement from the bank, an investment is not eligible for the insurance I just described above.

Let's review:

▲ *Insured:* Deposit accounts, including checking accounts, savings accounts, as well as money market deposit accounts (MMDAs) and certificates of deposit (CDs).

▲ *Not Insured:* Stock mutual fund, bond mutual fund, individual stock, individual bond, money market mutual fund. Pay particular attention to that last one: A money market mutual fund (MMMF) is not the same as a money market deposit account (MMDA). They look, smell, and behave the same in that both are designed to never lose a penny. But because an MMMF is a product created and run by a fund company—and not a bank—there is no insurance program. So in the extremely unlikely event that the mutual fund company runs into some sort of trouble—and I want to stress that this is *highly* unlikely to ever occur—there is a chance that you would not receive $1 for every dollar invested in an MMMF. Instead, your account might be nicked a few pennies for every dollar invested in the MMMF, whereas your bank MMDA would be fully insured as long as you meet the deposit limits described earlier.

MONTH ONE ACTION PLAN

✔ Open a new checking account that is free of monthly maintenance fees.

✔ Notify your employer to have your direct deposit sent to the new account. Same with any automatic payments or transfers you make from your checking account—notify everyone of the new account.

✔ Balance your checkbook each month; verify all your withdrawals and deposits, and keep track that every bill you pay is recorded as a debit on your account.

✔ Open a new savings or money market account that is FDIC insured and carries a high APY.

✔ Make it a goal to build a savings account over time that has a balance large enough to cover up to eight months of living expenses.

✔ Sign up for automatic deposits into your savings account.

✔ If you have more than $100,000 at any one institution, make sure you understand the rules for getting full insurance coverage.

FOLLOW THE PLAN TO SAVE YOURSELF

AN UNPRECEDENTED OFFER FROM TD AMERITRADE TO READERS OF WOMEN & MONEY

Having an account of your own is the absolute cornerstone of financial security. Without it, you cannot begin to build on a secure foundation. It is important for women as a practical matter, but it also has a critical, emotional effect as an essential tool of empowerment. I believe this so sincerely that I realized that I had to do everything in my power to make this happen and to turn this wish—that every woman have an account in her own name—into fact. I conceived of this as a national movement called **"Save Yourself,"** based on the simple premise that if every woman had a savings account in her own name, one day it might save her from a situation she may not want to be in.

In my search for an ally in this crusade, I approached TD AMERITRADE, a financial institution that I respect and trust one hundred percent, and asked for their help to make this wish a reality. The directors of TD AMERITRADE understood the significance of what was at stake and came up with an extraordinary offer, expressly for the readers of *Women & Money*.

HERE IS THE AMAZING OFFER TD AMERITRADE IS MAKING YOU TODAY AS A PART OF THE SAVE YOURSELF PLAN:

If you agree to open a brokerage account with TD AMERITRADE in your name and commit to an automatic deposit of at least $50 per month for twelve consecutive months, TD AMERITRADE will provide the incentive in the form of a $100 contribution into your account, to be made after your twelfth deposit. In other words, you save $600 or more over the course of a year and TD AMERITRADE will reward that effort with an extra

$100 deposit into your account. And that's in addition to the interest your money earns over the course of that year.

When you open your TD AMERITRADE account, your cash will be held in a money market deposit account (MMDA) that meets all of the requirements of a solid savings account covered in this month's plan:

- The MMDA is FDIC-insured.
- It pays a competitive interest rate, unique to this offer.
- There are no maintenance or annual fees.

Here's how it works:

1. Go to www.saveyourselfplan.com between 2/27/07 and 3/31/08.

2. Enter the Save Yourself offer code found on the special offer card at the back of this book. You'll then be taken to a page that contains the full details of this offer.

3. Click on the link to open a new TD AMERITRADE (non-retirement) account.

4. Arrange for a direct deposit of at least $50 per month into the account for twelve consecutive months. The first $50 must be deposited within 30 days of opening the account. You will earn a competitive interest rate on your deposits.

5. At the end of one year, TD AMERITRADE will deposit a $100 cash bonus into your account.

6. Should you need to withdraw the money prior to the twelve-month commitment, you may withdraw all of your deposits, plus the interest earned. However, you will forfeit the $100 bonus.

Of course, what TD AMERITRADE and I are hoping is that you will see how money grows and you'll be inspired to continue saving money every month and eventually go from being a saver to an investor. We hope you will want to deposit more than $50 a month, that you will increase the amount of these contributions and set goals for yourself that are in keeping with my advice on building an emergency fund and other savings objectives you may have. Becoming an investor is certainly the path I am urging you to follow in The Save Yourself Plan in the months ahead.

I also believe that saving and investing with TD AMERITRADE is a great decision. They are one of the best brokerage houses out there, and there is not a financial advisor in the country that would dispute this fact.

This is an incredible offer. Obviously, TD AMERITRADE cannot make this an open-ended deal, which is why you have to open your account prior to March 31, 2008. I hope you will tell every woman you know about this offer. Please join me in this nationwide movement to Save Yourself.

MONTH TWO:
Credit Cards and
FICO Credit Scores

I WOULD BE THRILLED IF YOU . . .

. . . Had one credit card that is in your name only.

. . . Checked every credit card statement every month.

. . . Avoided extra fees and higher interest rates on your credit cards.

. . . Aimed to pay your credit card bills in full each month.

. . . Knew the difference between good debt and bad debt.

. . . Committed to a strategy for paying off old credit card balances.

. . . Understood the importance of a good FICO credit score in your financial life.

. . . Got your FICO score.

. . . Learned how your credit reports work.

. . . Checked your credit reports annually.

I know credit cards are a major area of stress for so many of you. The ease of whipping out your card to pay for things makes self-restraint hard. Then the monthly bill comes and remorse sets in. Opening the statement and checking the current balance triggers massive pangs of guilt and panic. You had no idea that you charged *that much,* and you don't have the money in your checking account to pay off the entire balance. This begins the downward spiral of paying less than the entire bill and being charged interest on everything you don't pay off. Soon you find yourself in credit card hell, and the company that gave you the credit card (I'll refer to them as the card issuer from now on) couldn't be happier. This is exactly what they want to happen: Credit card companies make money when you can't pay off your entire bill in full. And once they have you in the hole—well, to be honest, you put yourself there—they certainly don't make it easy to dig yourself out.

This month's plan is all about learning how to use credit cards so they add to your financial power, rather than diminish it. We are going to begin with the most important step: making sure you have a credit card for yourself and only yourself. Then I will show you how to read your monthly statement and decipher all the terms and codes so you have control over your credit card, not vice versa. I am confident that knowledge will give you the power to avoid future credit card debt you can't afford. But I also realize that many of you already have some hefty card debt, often spread across multiple cards, and you don't know how or where to start dealing with it all. So included in this month's plan is an easy-to-grasp and easy-to-execute plan for taking control of your credit card debt.

Becoming a credit card expert will also help you build a stronger FICO credit score. As far as I'm concerned, your financial destiny goes nowhere without a good FICO credit score, and yet I know many of you aren't even aware of what a FICO credit score is, or the fact that you currently have three FICO credit scores that are playing a major role in your financial life.

Let's start by making sure you have financial muscle in your wallet: a credit card that is solely in your name.

GIVE YOURSELF—AND ONLY YOURSELF— SOME CREDIT

It's fine to have joint credit cards with your spouse or partner, but I also want you to have and use a credit card that is yours alone. You are never to let anyone else use that card—do you hear me?! Not even an authorized user. I need to be blunt here: I wish you all the happiness in the world, but no happiness is guaranteed. One day you could end up solo. And believe it or not, if you never had a credit card of your own, you may find it difficult to get one. And because you didn't have your own credit card, you may find it hard to rent an apartment or get a mortgage, a car loan, or any other type of credit by yourself. Sound crazy? Well, it has to do with creating a strong individual financial profile. How we handle our credit cards and our debt payments is considered a great window into seeing how financially responsible we are. This profile is known as your FICO credit score. I will explain how it works in detail just a few pages ahead, but the task at hand is to open a credit card account in your name only so you can begin to build a financial profile that is all yours. That is the start of your own financial power. And once you have the card, I want you to use it at least once a month and pay the entire bill on time every month. That is the best way to build a fabulous *individual* financial profile.

If you currently have a paying job and have a joint credit card, you should be able to get a credit card that is just in your name. You can shop for good card deals at www.bankrate.com and www.cardweb.com.

Card Shopping Tips

▲ **Don't pay an annual fee.** Your best bet is to get a card that is 100 percent free. Don't fall for the cards that offer you a great "rewards" program but also slide in a $75 or higher annual "membership" fee.

▲ **Make sure there is at least a three-week grace period.** The grace period is the time between the end of your monthly billing cycle and when your payment is due. You want to make sure a card has a grace period—not every card does—and that if you pay your bill in full on time, you will owe no interest. If you don't have a grace period, the card company can start charging you interest from the day you make a purchase, even if you do not have a prior month's balance.

▲ **Aim for a low interest rate . . . just in case.** If you pay off your bill in full each month, you avoid paying interest. But just in case you slip up—or have an emergency you can't cover from your savings account—I want you to make sure that the interest rate you will be charged for any card balance you don't pay off in full is as low as possible. So look for the card with the lowest interest rate. And pay attention to the fine print: Often card companies will offer a great introductory rate for a few months, but then your normal rate is boosted to 18 percent or more. Ideally, your permanent rate should be 10 percent or less. (The rate you will qualify for is largely dependent on your FICO credit score; with a good FICO credit score you should be able to get a low-rate credit card. You will learn how this works in this month of the plan.) And don't ever fall for the come-on that the advertised rate on the card is a "fixed rate." This is just one of endless ways credit card issuers love to confuse consumers. No matter what you hear, there is no true fixed-rate credit card. A credit-card issuer need only notify you thirty days in advance of any change to boost your interest rate. Typically, the bad news is in small print in one of those flimsy single-space inserts to your credit card statement that you never read.

▲ **Another tricky card game is how the interest on your balance is calculated. If your card issuer uses the two-cycle billing system and you tend to have an unpaid balance from time to time, you can end up paying a lot more than you anticipate. Details are on my website.**

Secured Credit

If you can't qualify for a credit card, I want you to start with what is known as a secured credit card. A secured card is a stepping-stone to getting a regular credit card.

A secured credit card works a bit differently from a regular credit card. To open the account, you must send the credit card company a deposit—say, $500 or so. You will not be allowed to charge more on your card than what you have on deposit. You see how this works: Your charges are "secured" by your deposit. That is, the credit card company has no risk of losing money if you don't pay your bill; they will simply take it out of your deposit.

Secured-Card Shopping Tips

You can shop for secured cards at www.bankrate.com and www.cardweb.com; if you belong to a credit union, ask if they offer secured cards.

▲ **Get a low annual fee.** Most secured cards charge an annual fee. Obviously, lower is better.
▲ **Make sure your payments are reported to a credit bureau.** This is the most important step in choosing a secured credit card. The reason you are opting for a secured card is that

you couldn't qualify for your own credit card. Most likely that was because you don't have a personal report card at any of the credit bureaus. So the whole purpose of the secured card is to start building up a "record" at the credit bureaus; all that means is that a credit bureau has a record of whether you pay your bills on time. But for that to happen, the company that gives you your secured card must send a report of your payments to at least one of the three credit bureaus: Equifax, Experian, or TransUnion. And not all secured-card companies do this reporting. So first you need to check that your secured card "reports" to one of those credit bureaus. You will need to call customer service to get this information.

Once you have the secured card, use it; make charges—it works just like a credit card at every store—and make sure you pay the bill on time. Every payment you make will be reported to the credit bureau; this is how you build a credit profile. After six months, you should check with the credit bureaus to make sure that your payment information is in fact being reported. Within a year or so of using your secured card responsibly, you will in fact have a "record" at the credit bureaus that should make it possible for you to qualify for a regular credit card. Again, please remember the reason you are doing this is to establish a good record so you can have a good FICO score. So the key is to make sure you pay your balance on the secured card in full each month and that you are never late with a payment.

A Debit Card Is Not a Credit Card or a Secured Credit Card!

When you make a purchase using your bank ATM card, the amount of the purchase is instantly deducted (debited) from your bank account balance. This is what is known as a debit card transaction. It is important to understand that purchases you make with a debit card are not reported to the credit bureaus; they do absolutely nothing to help build a profile. Please do not rely solely on a debit card. You must have your own bona fide card.

Now let's talk about how to handle regular credit cards.

Deciphering Your Credit Card Statement

Well, first you have to open it up. . . . I'm not kidding—the first step is to open the statement, whether you get it in the mail or read it online. Those of you who have practiced avoidance and denial in the past know this struggle all too well. Please stop beating yourself up. I don't care how bad it all looks today. The new you is all about taking control, starting now. If we have to dig you out of some serious credit card debt, that's what we're going to do. No shame, no blame, remember? Past is past. Let's focus on what you can do to make your future secure.

As we discussed in Month One, all your bills are to be opened immediately when they arrive, be it in the mail or online. Remember: Control = Taking Responsibility. And you really need to stay organized with your credit card bills. The basic task of making sure you send in your payment on time—even a small amount—is one of the strongest moves you can make. A payment that arrives one day late can cost you a fee of $39 and can drive your interest rate up.

So we're agreed: Taking control of your credit card means opening the statement right when it arrives. For the purpose of this month's exercise, please pull out your most recent statements. And here's the new routine you are to go through every month, with every credit card statement:

▲ **Scour your statement.** Verify that you indeed made every charge on the statement. If there are charges you didn't authorize, you may be a victim of identify theft—that is, someone has gained access to your credit card info and rung up charges on your account. Don't worry; you won't be held accountable for the charges as long as you report the problem to your credit card issuer immediately.

▲ **Go to my website for more information on what to do if you think you are a victim of identify theft.**

▲ **Check that any credits you are entitled to—for returned purchases, canceled memberships, or faulty charges— were in fact made to your account.** Don't assume, confirm! It is so easy to throw away hundreds of dollars a year by simply not spending two minutes a month scanning your credit card statement.

▲ **Notice the payment due date.** This is an easy trap to fall into. The due date is when your credit card issuer must receive your payment. It is not the date you must put the payment in the mail or authorize the online payment. It is the date your payment arrives at the card company. If you pay by mail, I want you to get that check in the mail at least **five business days before the due date**. If you use online payment, give yourself a lead time of at least **two business days**, just to be safe. What's the big deal? Well, for starters there's that issue of the late fee, which as I mentioned can run nearly $40—just for being one day late. But the potentially bigger problem is that being one day late on one credit card payment can cause the interest rate you are charged on that card, as well as any other card, to go up. This is one of those nasty tricks the card companies bury in the small print. If you are even just a day late, you can be labeled as being in "universal default," which gives every card company the right to increase the interest rate on your cards. Beat the payment due date—it's a simple way to keep money in your hands, not the credit card company's.

▲ **Find the minimum payment due on your bill.** This is the big bait the credit card issuer hopes you bite on. Remember, the card issuer makes money if you don't pay the bill in full; if you pay just the minimum amount that is due for the month, the card company gets to start charging you interest on the balance left unpaid. It's also important to understand that the minimum payment due typically represents just 3 percent or so of your total bill. So you are leaving 97 percent unpaid. Even if you vow to stop adding to your card balance but you just keep making the minimum payment due each month, you will end up needing years, and potentially thousands of dollars, to cover the interest you are charged each month on that big unpaid balance you are slowly whittling away at.

Before I show you an example of how it adds up, let's talk about that interest rate. The credit card company hopes you just pay attention to the **annual percentage rate (APR)** listed on your statement; this is the base interest rate for your unpaid balance. The average APR is around 15 percent, with many cards charging 22 percent or even more. But the actual interest rate you will get hit with is going to be slightly higher than the APR (in the vicinity of one to two percentage points more) if you carry an unpaid balance from month to month. It has to do with the math used by the credit card company in computing your interest. It's obviously in the credit card company's interest to downplay the interest rate, so that's why they show only the APR on your statement.

I am not going to insist you become an expert in how it all works. All I want is for you to understand that if you carry a balance, the actual interest rate you end up paying is slightly higher than the APR rate you see on your statement—maybe one to two percentage points more.

▲ **On my website I have a calculator where you tell me your credit card APR and I do the crazy math for you and tell you the real interest rate you will end up paying.**

Avoid the Minimum-Payment Trap

Now we're ready for an example. Let's say you have a $2,500 credit card bill this month and the true interest rate you pay is 16 percent. I am also assuming that you opt to pay just the minimum payment due, which will be 3 percent of your balance. If you take the card issuer's bait and just make the minimum payment due, you will end up paying $1,844 in interest over the course of the nearly fourteen years—yes, fourteen years!—it will take to get that balance completely paid off. Another way of looking at this is that you spent $2,500 but end up paying the credit card company a total of $4,344 ($2,500 + $1,844), or about 74 percent more than what you originally spent. If you happen to have $10,000 in credit card debt, the numbers get even uglier: It will take you more than twenty years to get your balance paid off, and in the process you will have paid the credit card company an extra $7,843 in interest.

▲ **On my website is a calculator that will tell you how long it will take to pay off your credit card bill, including the total interest you will owe if you opt to pay just the minimum amount due each month.**

Please do not to fall into this credit card trap. Control over your financial destiny means paying off the credit card balance each month. That should always be your goal. If you currently have an unpaid balance, I want you to make a commitment today not to add to it anymore. From this point forward, your goal is to pay off that debt.

Debt: Good vs. Bad

As much as I don't like credit card debt, I want you to understand that not all debt is bad. Unless you have inherited a bundle, make a bundle, or won a bundle in the lottery, you no doubt need to borrow money from time to time. That's fine, as long as you are careful about why and when you take out loans. It's what I call the good debt/bad debt test. And it is remarkably simple to follow.

Good debt is money you borrow to finance an asset. An asset is something that has value today and is expected to rise in value over time. A mortgage is a great example of good debt: You borrow money, and pay interest on that money, but you are getting a tax break on those interest payments. And whether you decide to stay in this house forever or sell it, the hope is that it will appreciate in value and turn out to have been a good investment. A student loan is also my idea of good debt. The asset is your (or your child's) future. More knowledge leads to higher earning power.

Bad debt is any money you borrow that is not used to finance an asset. Credit card debt is the ultimate in bad debt. (The only exception is if you use it for the absolute necessities—needs, not desires—when you are young and struggling to make ends meet.) Card debt to pay for spa treatments, dinners out, the latest shoes or handbags that you want but really don't need is bad debt. Taking out a home-equity line of credit to finance a vacation is more bad debt.

So, too, is a car loan. I bet that might surprise you. Here's the deal: Your car's value never rises. It always falls. This is known as depreciation. So borrowing money to pay for a car isn't as smart as borrowing money to buy a home. However, I understand that most of you need to take out a loan to buy a car. Try to minimize how much car debt you have and aim to pay it off as quickly as possible; in my opinion, you never want to take more than three years to pay off a car loan. (And please, do not ever lease a car; the leasing process makes it inevitable that you will never be in control of your car finances.)

 To learn more about why I never recommend car leasing over traditional car loans, please go to my website.

Sort Your Debt

I want you to take a look at your current debts and sort them into **good** and **bad**. Obviously, the objective is to minimize your bad debts. Next, we will walk through what to do with the ultimate in bad debt: your unpaid credit card balances. But I also want you to keep the good/bad strategy in mind when you are contemplating taking on new debt. Always ask yourself: Is it good debt, or is it bad?

Dealing with Unpaid Credit Card Balances

If you do not have any unpaid credit card bills, God bless you— jump ahead to the section on credit scores.

If you do have unpaid credit card balances, it is important that you stop looking at it as a sign of failure, or with such great guilt that you are too fearful and ashamed to take control. I want you to keep reminding yourself that what happened in the past is out of your control, but what you choose to make of your future is completely within your control. So how about we focus on giving you a strategy for creating a future that is free of credit card debt?

That starts with a commitment to use your card responsibly. My definition of responsibly is keeping your regular monthly charges limited to what you can pay off in full when the bill arrives. The only charges you should allow yourself to make that you won't be able to pay off are for true emergencies that you can't cover out of your savings account. This is going to involve adding "no" to your spending vocabulary. You need to say it to yourself, your partner, probably your kids. And it isn't easy. But I want you to keep coming back to why you are reading this book: You want control of your financial life. That takes a commitment to making wise choices. And I am hard-pressed to imagine a wiser choice than avoiding high credit card balances that come with high interest-rate charges.

Now, about all the "old" credit card debt you've already rung up. Below are a series of strategies. The order is intentional; if the first strategy doesn't make sense for you, move on to step 2, and so on.

These strategies are based on what makes best financial sense. That said, I recognize that debt, especially credit card debt, can have a huge emotional impact on women. If nothing would bring you a greater sense of relief or power than to know you have paid off your credit card balance—regardless of whether it is the smartest financial move—then that is exactly what you should do. However, I want to make sure that you do not go from one bad situation to another. So in the box below is first what not to do in paying off your credit card debt, followed by what I do want you to do.

NEVER USE HOME EQUITY TO GET RID OF CREDIT CARD DEBT

There is no shortage of advertisements promising to solve your credit card problems by helping you take out a loan against your house. The come-on is enticing; the interest rate on your home equity line of credit (HELOC) will typically be a lot lower than the interest you pay on your credit card, and lenders are quick to point out that interest payments on HELOCs can be tax-deductible.

Don't fall for it.

I never want you to "tap" your home equity to pay off your credit card bill.

Your credit card debt is what is known as "unsecured debt"—that is, you didn't put up any money or asset of yours as collateral. A HELOC is a "secured" debt: When you have a HELOC, your home is your collateral. If you are unable to keep up with your HELOC payments, the lender has the right to seek payment by using the collateral. Translation: You could be forced to sell your home to make good on your HELOC debt. It simply does not make sense to transfer unsecured debt (credit card) to a secured debt (your home; HELOC). Why would you want to put your home at risk to pay off the credit card bills?

The HELOC strategy also harbors a dangerous trap: I have seen so many women pay off their credit card balances with the money from a HELOC and then turn around and run up huge new balances on their credit cards—the very same credit cards they just tried to clean up with the HELOC. So that leaves them with the HELOC debt to pay off *and* all the new debt on their credit cards—and it puts them in worse financial shape than before! Please, do not ever use a HELOC to pay off your credit card debt. And I mean never.

STRATEGIES FOR PAYING OFF CREDIT CARD DEBT

Transfer Your Balance to a New Card with a Low Interest Rate

If you are paying more than 10 percent APR on your current credit card balances, I want you to look into transferring all the money to a new card that charges you a lower APR. This is what is known as a balance transfer. Many card issuers will offer you an initial APR on a balance transfer that can be as low as zero percent for the first year. Not everyone is going to qualify for that great deal, so you need to shop around to find the best deal given your current financial situation.

You can search for balance-transfer credit card deals at www. find-cards-now.com.

If you do manage to get a zero-rate or low-rate card, great! But please be extra careful in how you treat that new card. The card issuer is going to be working just as hard to get you to trip up on your payments so it can jack up the interest rate. The most important step for you is to be superdiligent about getting your payments in on time. Not just on this card, but on every bill you owe. As I explained earlier, credit card companies use a policy known as "universal default": If you are late making a payment on any other credit card, you can lose the great rate on a card you have paid on time.

In fact, I don't even want you to carry that card in your wallet. Why? Because the great zero percent rate or low rate you are given on transfers often does not apply to new purchases you make with that card. The same card that charges you zero percent on the money you transfer often will charge you 18 percent or more on new charges. And don't think you can just pay off that new charge ASAP. The card issuer is one step ahead of you; it will make sure you end up paying that high interest rate. If you use your transfer card for a new charge, when you send in your payment the card issuer will use that money to reduce your transfer balance (which the card issuer is earning zero interest on) rather than apply your payment to the balance on your new charges. That means you now have a new unpaid balance on the new charges, and that means paying interest on that balance. The card issuer wins again! You are now paying 18 percent or more on your new charge balance. And until you get your transfer balance completely erased, you are not going to be able to pay off the new balance.

Pay Attention to Transfer Fees

Make sure you read the fine print and understand the cost of moving your money. It rarely is free. Many card issuers will charge a fee equal to 3 percent of the transfer amount, but they cap the fee at $75 or so. But some issuers do not cap the fee; it can be a flat 3 percent of the total transfer amount. So if you transfer $10,000, a card with a cap might charge you $75 or so, but the card without the fee cap is going to charge you $300. That's a big difference.

Now, I realize the temptation may be to just make the minimum payment each month on the new card, since you have such a great rate. I want you to get out of that mind-set. First, the great rate is usually good only for an introductory period; after that time, the rate typically shoots up to 15–18 percent or more. Sure, you can do yet another transfer to another card, but if you keep opening new cards it can have a negative effect on your FICO credit score; I don't recommend opening more than one card a year. Besides, in keeping with our "take charge" attitude, the better approach is to do everything you can to pay off the debt as quickly as possible. That means paying as much each month as you can. It is up to you to determine what that level is. Push yourself here. If it's easy to send in $50 more than the minimum payment due, push yourself to send in $100. If $100 is a snap, see where you can scale back on your spending to send in $200. The quicker you get rid of this debt, the sooner you are going to feel in control of your financial destiny. (One important note: I hope this is obvious, but I want to make sure that you never generate extra money for your credit card bills by falling behind on other financial bills. You must pay your utilities, rent, phone bills, and so forth, on time. Do not shortchange those bills in an effort to come up with more for your credit card payment.)

If you still have an unpaid balance after the great intro rate expires, you should do another balance transfer to a new card.

However, do not exceed more than one transfer a year so you don't mess up your FICO credit score by opening more than one new card a year.

Consider Tapping Your Savings Account to Reduce (or Eliminate) Your Credit Card Debt

Here's a basic math lesson to keep in mind whenever you are weighing your financial choices: Always ask yourself if what you are earning in interest is more or less than what you are paying in interest. So let's say you are earning 5 percent on your savings account but you are paying 16 percent on your credit card balance. Hmmm . . . you're 11 percentage points down by my math. And to be totally clear, the 5 percent you are earning on your savings is actually money that is taxed, so what you are really earning after paying tax is going to be less than 5 percent. So that makes the real gap between your after-tax earnings on your savings and the interest you pay on your credit cards even bigger.

Rule of Thumb: If the interest rate on your credit card is at least four percentage points higher than the interest rate on your savings account, it makes financial sense to use your savings to pay off or reduce your credit card debt.

And don't think you are mortgaging your financial security by using up your emergency cash fund; the reality is that as long as you have credit card debt you don't really have true financial security in the first place.

Commit to a Systematic Pay-Back Strategy: Pay More Each Month on the Card with the Highest Interest Rate

Pull out all your statements for all your cards. First we need to have a reality check: Add up all your unpaid balances on all your credit cards.

Unpaid Balance

Card 1

Card 2

Card 3

Total Amount Due

Take a look at that balance. I am not trying to make you feel bad. I want you to get angry: angry that you have let yourself get into this most powerless of positions. Angry enough to motivate you to vow that today is when you start to exercise control over your credit cards. Yes, it is going to take time to wipe out the card debt; but as long as you are moving in the right direction, you are in charge.

I want you to arrange your credit card statements by organizing them according to their APR: The card with the highest APR comes first; the card with the lowest APR is last. Fill in the chart below.

Minimum Payment Due   **APR**

Card 1

Card 2

Card 3

**Total of Monthly
Minimum Payments Due**

Each month you obviously need to make the minimum payment due on each credit card, but the objective, once again, is to send in more than the minimum due on the one card that charges you the highest APR. I don't care if another card has a bigger balance; your focus is on the card with the highest APR. Again, I am leaving it up to you to determine how much extra you can send in on that highest-rate card. It's up to you to decide how much power you want to exert: The more you commit to paying each month, the more power to you. It's that simple.

And here's a tip for outsmarting the card companies: Each month your card issuer is going to recalculate your minimum payment due based on your current (lower) balance. You are simply charged a flat percent of your outstanding balance. Let's say it is 3 percent. Every month as your balance decreases, so, too, will your minimum payment due, because it is always going to be 3 percent of whatever the balance is. This is how the credit card companies string out your repayment period; the card company wants to keep you paying interest for as long as possible. So here's how to avoid that trap: Take a look at your monthly minimum due this month on your highest-rate card. Then decide what you intend to add to it. You are to pay at least that amount every month going forward. Don't pay anything less, even though your statement will indeed show a lower minimum payment due in subsequent months. Ignore it. Just stick with what you paid in the first month of your payback plan. If you can afford it the first month, you can afford it every month. So let's say your minimum payment due this month on your highest-rate card is $75 and you decide you can add $50 to that amount. Your total payment on that card will be $125 this month. I want you always to pay at least $125 a month until you have completely wiped out the debt on that card, no matter what smaller amount is listed as your minimum payment due.

Once you get that highest-rate card paid off, I want you to focus on boosting your payments on the card with the next-highest APR. The extra payment you make each month on this card should be equal to the entire amount you were sending in on the card that previously had the highest APR. So, going back to our example, if you were paying $125 on the highest-rate card and then you finally paid it off, you are to then take that $125 a month and apply it to the next card on your hit list. I know you can afford it; after all, you were just paying $125 a month on the first card. The $125 is to be added to whatever minimum payment you were making on the second card. Then, once the second card is paid off, take the total monthly payment on card 2 and apply it to card 3. And keep at it until you have all your credit card debt paid off. It may take you six months or six years. The power is in knowing you are on a path to wiping out the expensive debt no matter how long it takes.

 If you are in serious credit card debt and do not feel that any of the strategies I discuss below will help you, please go to my website for more information on how to find a good debt-counseling service to help you.

BEWARE OF CASH ADVANCES

The biggest mistake you can ever make with a credit card is to use it to get a cash advance. You will be charged a fee for the money—it can be about 3 percent of your withdrawn amount—and interest on the money you were "advanced" from the day you took the money, even if you do not have any unpaid balance on the card. That's a bit different from how your regular charges work on your card. With regular charges, you do not owe interest as long as you pay your bill (in full) by the due date. Make your payment in full within this grace period and you owe no interest. But there is no grace period for cash advances. Even worse, the interest rate is typically 22 percent or more. That's insane. Now, if you somehow find yourself in an impossible situation where you feel your only option is to take out a cash advance, my recommendation is to see if you can qualify for a balance transfer to a new credit card with a low introductory rate, and move the cash advance balance to that new card.

How Many Is Too Many?

If you have more than a few credit cards and you have gotten into trouble running up unpaid balances on those cards, you need a better card-management strategy.

You should always have two credit cards—one for regular use and one as backup. *One* for backup, not ten. And if your wallet is full of department store cards, you are to get them out of there right now. Those cards are just bad news. Now, I know what happened: You were at the cash register when you were offered 10 percent off your purchase if you opened the account, so you signed on the dotted line. Even worse, you probably went and bought something else just to "make the most" of that 10 percent deal. But saving 10 percent once can end up costing you a ton: If you don't pay off the entire bill when it arrives, you are typically smacked with a high interest rate—20 percent or more for many stores.

The simplest solution is that once you get the balances paid off, stop using those high-interest-rate cards. Put them in a drawer or a safety-deposit box, or just take a pair of scissors to them if that's what it takes to not use them.

Your best move is to not cancel the card; doing that can have a negative impact on your FICO credit score. That said, if you happen to pay annual fees on those cards, then I do think it can make sense to cancel them—but do it carefully. Here's how: Arrange the fee cards in ascending order of their credit limits. I want you first to cancel the card with the lowest credit limit. A year later, you can cancel the card with the next-lowest credit limit. Keep this up—canceling just one card a year—until you are rid of the cards with annual fees. Just ahead is a full explanation of why canceling can be a tricky move, and how your credit limit is an important factor in determining your FICO credit score.

WHAT A FICO CREDIT SCORE IS AND
WHY IT MATTERS . . . A LOT

If you had a choice, you'd want to be in a position to get the best financing deals for credit cards and loans, correct? The less interest you have to pay, the more money you have to spend and save for yourself and your family. Well, I'm here to tell you that you do indeed have a choice. What you end up paying in interest on credit cards, mortgages, and car loans is largely dependent on your FICO credit score. I am guessing that a lot of you vaguely recognize the term "credit score" but have no real idea what it is and what it means to you.

Whether you know it or not, just about every bill you pay is tracked by three credit bureaus: Equifax, Experian, and Trans-Union. They each have a massive file on how good you are at paying your bills on time and how much debt you have. The information in your personal financial file is then thrown into a black box that uses all sorts of mathematical formulas to spit out a personal score for you. That score is known as a credit score, and the company that pioneered this credit score is the Fair Isaac Corporation—FICO for short. When you apply for a credit card or any type of loan, your FICO credit score is a quick take on how responsible you are with your debt. It tells the lender at a glance whether you are a good person to do business with. If you have a great score—meaning you are superconscientious about paying your bills and aren't drowning in bad debt—lenders will offer you their best deals. That can mean a lower interest rate on your mortgage, car loan, or credit cards. And just to totally throw you for a loop: Your FICO credit score can make or break getting a new job. Some employers (with your permission) will check your FICO credit score to get a handle on how responsible you are. Landlords often rely on credit scores, too; they will screen out renters with bad credit scores. And your credit record can also be used to generate another type of score that is often used to set your auto insurance premium.

Bottom line: You better know your score.

Why FICO Is the Best Score

There are many companies that compute your credit score, but as far as I am concerned you should pay only for what is known as your FICO credit score. As I said before, this is a score created by the company Fair Isaac, which pioneered the credit score. **Full disclosure:** I have a business agreement with Fair Isaac (*Suze Orman's FICO Kit*), but I do not receive one penny when you purchase an individual FICO credit score, which is all I am going to insist you do. The reason I work with Fair Isaac is the same reason I want you to use them for your credit score: They are the gold standard. The vast majority of credit card companies and mortgage lenders and other companies interested in your credit profile use the FICO credit score when they size up your credit-worthiness. If that's the one they are checking, that is the one you better check to make sure your credit is in good shape. It makes little sense to check some other company's score if your lender—or landlord, or potential employer—is likely to be using the FICO score.

How to Get Your FICO Credit Score

You can get your FICO credit score at www.myfico.com. In fact, you have three separate FICO scores—one based on each of your financial files at the three main credit bureaus. But there's no need to pay for all three scores unless you are about to take out a new mortgage. For our purposes now, it's fine to just get one score. The regular fee is $15.95 per score.

▲ **On my website you can check to see if myfico.com is offering a discount to *Women & Money* readers for my FICO KIT, which contains three prepaid FICO scores and personalized computer coaching where I help you get the best deal on buying a home and car, as well as give you a personalized program for getting out of credit card debt.**

FICO credit scores range from 300 to 850, the higher the better. Generally, if your score is at least 760 you are in great shape; that is currently the "top tier" of the ranking system and means that you will have a great chance to qualify for the best loans and deals. (The cutoffs for the different tiers of FICO scores is actually determined by the lenders who use the scores. These ranges can change from time to time, but they tend to stay in line with their historical norms.)

▲ **If your FICO score is below 760, go to my website for strategies that will help you boost your FICO score.**

The computation of your FICO credit score is based on five factors. I want to focus on the two most important ones: paying your bills on time and how much you owe. These two elements account for a combined 65 percent of your FICO credit score. The three other factors (how long you have had credit; whether you have recently applied for a lot of new credit; and your "mix" of credit, such as credit cards, car loans, and student loans) account for just 35 percent.

Now you understand why I was making such a big deal about timely payments: It's a huge part of your FICO score. And it only needs to be the minimum payment due.

Boost Your FICO Credit Score by Lowering Your Overall Debt

The other major element of your FICO credit score is how much you owe. A key factor in this part of your score is known as your debt-to-credit-limit ratio. This is computed partially by adding up all your outstanding credit card debt and dividing it by your total credit limits on all your cards. So let's say you have $1,500 in unpaid credit card debt on three cards and your available credit limits on the three cards are $3,000, $5,000, and $7,000, for a combined total of $15,000. Here's the math: total debt ÷ total available credit. So in this example, $1,500 ÷ $15,000. That gives you a debt-to-credit-limit ratio of 10 percent. There is no set-in-stone rule about what constitutes a good ratio, but obviously, the lower the better. A ratio of 50 percent is not nearly as good as a ratio of 10 percent.

You can easily estimate your ratio by adding up your total unpaid balances and dividing them by your total credit limit. If you have a high ratio, chances are your FICO score may not be in the 760+ club. The best way to change that is to focus on reducing your unpaid balances. As you bring down the debt part of the equation, your debt-to-credit-limit ratio will also fall. When your debt-to-credit-limit ratio falls, your FICO credit score should go up.

The debt-to-credit-limit calculation is why I don't recommend canceling unused credit cards if you have unpaid balances. When you cancel the card, your "available credit" will be reduced by whatever amount you had on that card, so you could inadvertently cause your ratio to get bigger.

Check Your Credit Report

Because your FICO credit score is based on the information the three credit bureaus have on you, you also need to check that the credit bureaus have their facts straight. And I have to tell you, they often don't. Mistakes about your payment history, your address, and mixing you up completely with someone else are all too common. Checking your credit report is also the best line of defense in catching anyone who has stolen your identity and created bogus credit card accounts or taken out a loan using your name and information.

You may have seen all sorts of ads offering you a "free" credit check. Be very careful: These are free only if you sign up for additional services that cost you money.

How to Get Your Credit Reports for Free

The only way to get a truly free credit report is to go to www.annualcreditreport.com or by calling (877) 322–8228. By law, each of the three credit bureaus must give you a free credit report once a year. If you find any erroneous information, you will need to contact the credit bureau and file a challenge; the bureau you contact is required to pass along your information to the other two bureaus.

 I wish I could tell you that fixing mistakes on your credit report is a snap, but it isn't. On my website are detailed instructions and contact information for how to correct mistakes on your credit report, as well as how to report any instance of identity theft.

ACTION PLAN: SUMMARY FOR CREDIT CARDS AND FICO CREDIT SCORES

✔ Make sure you have at least one credit card that is in your name only.

✔ If you can't initially qualify for a bank credit card, start with a secured credit card that reports your payments to a credit bureau.

✔ Read your monthly credit card statements when they arrive; check for mistakes and overbilling, and take note of the payment due date.

✔ Always get your payment in on time—*before* the due date. No excuses.

✔ Get serious about getting rid of old unpaid credit card balances.

   ~ If your credit card interest rate is higher than your savings account APY, use your savings account to pay off high-rate credit card balances.

   ~ Consider transferring unpaid balances to a new credit card that offers a low introductory rate.

   ~ Send in more than the minimum due on your card with the highest interest rate.

✔ Get your FICO credit score.

✔ Get three free credit reports annually at www.annual-creditreport.com.

Month Three:
Retirement Investing

I WOULD BE THRILLED IF YOU . . .

. . . Started saving something, anything, for your retirement.

. . . Understood that even a little today can add up to a lot tomorrow.

. . . Participated in your employer's retirement plan if they match your contribution.

. . . Qualified for the *maximum* employer match.

. . . Chose the right investments for your 401(k) or 403(b).

. . . Never took a loan from your 401(k) plan or cashed out your money before your retirement.

. . . Knew that Roth IRAs are an unbeatable retirement account.

. . . Understood that even stay-at-home moms or non-working spouses can have a spousal IRA.

> ... Committed to investing in an IRA in addition to investing in your 401(k) or 403(b).
> ... Opened up a Roth IRA or traditional IRA account at a discount brokerage firm or mutual fund company.
> ... Opened up a traditional IRA if you are currently ineligible for a Roth, with the intention of converting to a Roth in the future.
> ... Chose the right investments for your IRA.

Time to switch gears. In the first two months, we focused on spending and basic saving. That's the solid foundation for building financial security right here, right now. Next we're going to face the future and focus on investing money today so you can live comfortably in retirement.

The issues raised by the notion of saving for retirement are at the heart of Bag Lady Syndrome. It's all about the fear that you won't have enough money to keep a roof over your head when you are old. Panic invariably sets in once you come across an online calculator that spits out some terrifyingly huge number you need to have saved up for retirement, or a magazine article that tells you that if you aren't religiously socking away 15 percent of your income in retirement accounts you are doomed. As far as I am concerned, focusing on a big number is horrible retirement-planning advice. It is a total demotivator: When the news is that you need to climb Mt. Everest and you've yet to scale a molehill, it's not surprising that you become disheartened and demoralized.

So here's your first retirement savings task: Tune out the big number talk for now. I want you to *focus on what is actually in your power to control today:* doing the very best job possible of saving for your retirement. Whatever that amount is, it is the right amount, because it represents everything that you have the ability to give today.

This month we are going to concentrate on making sure you are taking advantage of special retirement accounts you may be eligible for. There's a lot of information ahead that you need to know in order to ground yourself and understand the moves I'm asking you to make. Remember, "not knowing" is no longer an acceptable excuse for inaction. So please don't be daunted by the amount of information I'm asking you to absorb; at the end of the day, the actions I'm prescribing are clear and simple and spelled out for you.

First you'll read about the retirement accounts offered through your employer, such as 401(k)s. Then we will walk through individual retirement accounts (IRAs) that you can—and should—invest in on your own. I will give you a simple plan for how to invest your retirement savings. That's another classic stumbling block for women: You let the money sit in cash because you can't figure out what the right investment moves are. That indecision will not help you reach your retirement goals. You need to make sure the money you can put away for your retirement has the chance to earn strong returns for you.

The only way to counteract feelings of helplessness, indecision, and defeatism is *to act. The most powerful attitude you can own when it comes to your future is self-reliance,* because when it comes to your retirement, it's really up to you to take care of you.

Very few companies today offer a traditional pension plan whereby employees are given a set payout when they retire based on a formula that takes their salary and years of service into account. And I have to be honest: Even if you happen to work for one of the dinosaurs still offering these plans, it is smart to save up on your own, too. So many large companies that have promised future pensions to current employees are beginning to balk at the cost of living up to those promises. They may end up scaling back retirement benefits or, in extreme cases, look to the federal government for some bailout assistance.

And please don't think that what you are currently paying into the Social Security system will be enough to cover your retirement needs. We all know that whatever your Social Security check will look like when the time comes, it will not be enough for you to live on no matter how large it is. Social Security was never meant to be the sole retirement plan for Americans. It was designed to serve as a financial safety net for those most in need, not a full-scale solution for all of us. Each year you should be receiving a statement in the mail from the Social Security Administration noting your earnings history and an estimate of your expected benefits in retirement. You can also use free online Social Security calculators to estimate your benefits on www.socialsecurity.gov/planners/calculators.htm.

So that brings us back to you and the need to save for yourself. Now, I know many of you can't imagine putting your retirement needs ahead of taking care of your kids' needs today or saving for their college education. So let me address that classic dilemma first.

SAVING FOR YOUR KIDS' COLLEGE VS. SAVING FOR YOUR RETIREMENT

I know every mother reading this wants to do everything she can for her children. That includes the wish to put her children through college. But I need you to read what I am about to tell you with an open mind: If you don't have enough money to save today for your kids' college funds *and* your own retirement, your retirement must take top billing. Not because you love your kids less, but because you love them best. The reality is that if you retire without ample money to support yourself, you will become a financial burden on your children. Remember the definition of generosity in "The 8 Qualities of a Wealthy Woman"? An act that is meant to be generous but that nonetheless erodes or diminishes the financial needs of the giver is not a true form of generosity. You have no idea how many e-mails I get from adult children who are worried about how their parents are ever going to make it. So understand that the most generous decision you can make today—for yourself and your children—is to build as much financial security as you can, so that down the line the only thing you ask your kids for is more time with them and the grandkids, not financial aid.

That doesn't mean you are leaving your kids out in the cold. As I like to say, there are plenty of loans for college but there are no loans for retirement. You need to approach this strategically: You and your children will make use of loans to help pay for their college, and in the meantime the money you have for long-term savings will be targeted for your retirement funds.

MAKE THE MOST OF TIME

One of the greatest misconceptions about investing is that it takes a lot of money to make a lot of money. That's simply not true. What it takes is some money and a lot of time. Time is a crucial component of investing, but it's one we tend to squander.

Let's look at two different scenarios: Mary starts to save for retirement when she is twenty-five. Dee waits until she is forty-five to get serious about saving up. They both commit to investing $200 a month and will earn an average annual return on their investment of 8 percent. That doesn't mean they will earn 8 percent every year, but that over many years their gains and losses will work out to an average return of 8 percent.

By the time Mary is forty-five years old, she has invested $48,000 of her own money and it has grown to nearly $119,000. Dee hasn't yet started saving.

At age forty-five:

Mary (starts investing at age twenty-five)		Dee (starts investing at age forty-five)	
Amount invested:	$48,000	Amount invested:	$0
Total value	**$118,589**	**Total value:**	**$0**

At age sixty-five:

Mary		Dee	
Amount invested:	$96,000	Amount invested:	$48,000
Total value:	**$702,856**	**Total value:**	**$118,589**

From the age of forty-five to sixty-five, Mary keeps up her investing plan and Dee finally starts hers. When they both reach age sixty-five, Mary has invested twice as much of her own money ($96,000) as Dee ($48,000). But look at the bottom line: Mary's retirement nest egg is nearly *six times* larger than Dee's: $702,856 compared to $118,589. Mary invested just $48,000 more than Dee but ends up with nearly $585,000 more. (For Dee to end up at sixty-five with the same $702,856 as Mary, she would have to invest nearly $1,200 a month beginning when she is forty-five.)

So what's Mary's trick? Nothing more than time. The earlier you start saving, the more time your money has to grow. When your money grows over time, you are taking advantage of what is known as compounding, or compound growth. The easiest way to explain this concept is with an example. Let's say you start with $1,000. And you earn 10 percent in the first year. That's $100. So you start the second year with $1,100. And let's once again assume you earn 10 percent. But it's now 10 percent of $1,100, not 10 percent of $1,000. So the second year you make $110, not $100. That brings your balance to $1,210 ($1,100 + $110 = $1,210). If you again earn a 10 percent return, you will make $121 in year three; you earn 10 percent on $1,210. This process of compounding, of earning interest on your interest, works just like a snowball rolling down a hill, getting bigger as it goes. And the longer your money has to snowball, the more money you will have in the long run. Compounding was what made Mary so much more successful than Dee.

Now, if you are already in your forties and fifties and haven't saved a dime, don't beat yourself up and don't give up. Remember, no shame, no blame for what you have and haven't done in the past. Focus on what is within your control: the choices you make today and every day going forward. That means starting to save—right here, right now. Make the most of the time you have before retirement, whether you are twenty-five or fifty-five.

FINDING MONEY

The other big lesson from Mary and Dee is that a small amount of money can make a big difference in your life. Mary ends up with more than $700,000 not by winning the lottery or waiting for a big bonus or inheritance, but by diligently socking away $200 a month. That's $50 a week. I bet that if you're seriously motivated to create your own financial security—and banish the bag lady fears—you will find a way to come up with $50 a week to put toward your savings.

On my website you will find a calculator that allows you to input what you think you can afford to save each month and will then show you what that money can grow to by the time you are sixty-five. I encourage you to use the calculator and try out different scenarios: Start with what you can easily afford to save each month. Then do another calculation increasing your monthly contribution by $25. Then again at $50. And what if you can manage to invest $100 more a month than you originally thought?

I suspect that many of you are saying that while those numbers all make sense to you, the truth is that you simply do not have any money left over, after paying your bills, to save for retirement. Okay, I hear that, but now I need you to hear me: If you do not have the money today to pay your bills while you have a paycheck coming in, how do you expect to pay those exact same bills later in life when you no longer have a paycheck coming in? The answer is you won't be able to. You have got to start saving, and you have got to start now. My experience is that once you make saving for retirement a priority and have money directly invested in retirement accounts from your paycheck, you end up simply spending less money. I want you to think about this. Isn't it true? The more money you make, the more money you spend? I thought so. So reverse that. The less money that ends up in your wallet or checking account, the less money you will spend. By having money directly deposited into a retirement account that will make your take-home less, the less you will spend. Is it that simple? You bet it is. So, to that end, we will start with retirement plans that are offered by employers to employees.

THE RETIREMENT PLAN OFFERED BY YOUR EMPLOYER

Chances are you have a retirement plan at work. What your plan is called depends on whom you work for. Corporations offer what is known as a 401(k) plan. If you work for a nonprofit, such as a school or hospital, it typically goes by the name 403(b); public employees have a type of 403(b) known as a tax-sheltered annuity (TSA), and the retirement plan for members of the military or civil servants is called a thrift savings plan (TSP).

Despite the different names, these retirement plans work in a similar fashion. You, the employee, designate how much of your paycheck—up to set maximums—goes into your retirement account. The money that you designate is automatically deducted from your paycheck and deposited into a retirement account. To keep things simple, when I refer to 401(k)s, I am also including 403(b)s, TSAs, and TSPs.

How Much Can Be Invested

In 2007, you can invest up to $15,500 in your 401(k). If you are over fifty years old, you are permitted an additional "catch-up" contribution of $5,000, for a total of $20,500. The contribution limits in 2008 and beyond will be increased to account for inflation. (Inflation is a measurement of how the cost of goods and services changes over time. When you hear that something is adjusted for inflation, be it what we can invest in our 401(k)s or the benefit we will receive from Social Security, it means the amount is changed to keep up with any rising costs in living expenses.)

The Tax Break Carrot

To encourage you to save, the traditional 401(k) plans have a bunch of tax breaks. First, the money you invest in the plan—known as your contribution—is taken out of your paycheck before taxes. So every dollar that you invest in your retirement plan reduces your taxable income for that year by $1. For example, if you make $40,000 a year but invest $3,000 in your retirement plan, your taxable income drops to $37,000; that means a lower tax bill for the year. As long as you keep your money inside the retirement plan, you won't owe any taxes. It is only when you start taking money out of the account that you will owe tax. This setup is known as tax-deferred investing; your money gets to grow and grow without any tax bill while it is invested. The tax bill is deferred, or postponed, until you are retired and withdrawing money from the account. In return for getting these nice breaks, you agree to keep the money invested until you reach retirement age, or you will be hit with a 10 percent early-withdrawal penalty. Generally, you must be at least 59½, though in a few instances you can withdraw money at age fifty-five without incurring the penalty. No matter what your age when you take money out of a 401(k) plan, you will owe tax on the amount of money that you take out.

The Employer Matching Contribution

As good as those tax breaks can be, the other reason every woman—or her spouse or partner—should invest in a 401(k) is to qualify for your employer's retirement bonus. In the majority of plans, your employer will kick in a contribution to your account as long as you invest some of your own money, too. This is called an employer matching contribution. In my opinion, it should be called a retirement bonus, because it is extra money your employer agrees to give you every year as long as you contribute to your 401(k). The formula for the match varies. Here's one example: An employer contributes 50 cents for every $1 an employee invests in her 401(k) account, up to a maximum of, say, $1,500. So in this example, if you invest $3,000 of your own money, your employer will add in another $1,500. That's an instant 50 percent gain! But if you don't contribute to the plan, you don't get the match. Which is really no different than telling your boss you don't want a bonus. And let me know the next time you come across an investment that pays off at 50 percent. Do you see how crazy it is to turn down free money?

Max Out on Your Retirement Bonus

If you—or your spouse or partner—is eligible for a 401(k) or other retirement plan that offers a match, you must take full advantage of it. Amazingly, about 20 percent of people who are enrolled in a 401(k) plan don't contribute enough to get the maximum matching contribution from their employer. Big mistake! How big? Let me show you. If you turned down a $1,500 matching contribution for twenty years and that money earned an average annual return of 8 percent, you would have turned your back on nearly $75,000.

If you just haven't bothered to sign up for the plan even though you are eligible, I want you to get on the phone with HR right away and start the paperwork. A new law passed by Congress in 2006 encourages companies to enroll employees in the retirement plan automatically unless the employee explicitly asks to opt out of the plan, but you still need to do a bit of legwork. When you are automatically enrolled in a plan, your employer chooses a contribution level for you—maybe 2 percent of your pay. The "default" contribution level your employer chooses for you might not be high enough to qualify for the maximum matching contribution. So it's up to you to check with HR to see if you need to boost what you pay into the plan so you can be assured you are getting the maximum "bonus" contribution from your employer.

Important Note: If your plan does not offer a match, I don't want you to make your 401(k) your first retirement move. Later in the plan for this month, I'll go into detail about Roth IRAs, which are a smarter choice for you, but I still want you to read the following sections so you can educate yourself on how 401(k) plans work.

Choose the Right Investments for Your Plan

Signing up for the plan is just step one; next you need to tell the plan how you want your money invested. You are usually limited to the choices offered within your plan. Typically, these are the stock of your company that you work for and mutual funds. Many companies have gone overboard and built retirement plans that have more than a dozen different mutual funds to choose from. I know that too much choice keeps many of you from even investing in the plan in the first place, so let me simplify it all for you.

WHAT IS A STOCK?

The first thing I want you to understand is the difference between a single stock and a mutual fund. When a company wants to raise money so that they can expand and grow, one way for them to do so is to create a specific number of shares of their company to sell to other people for a specific sum of money. This is called *going public*. That is, the public can buy stock in that company. When you own stock in a company, you are an equity shareholder of that company and you own a tiny piece of that company. That is why a share of stock can also be called an equity. If the company does well, the value of the shares will rise; if the company does not do well, the share price will go down. The share of a company that has gone public is traded on a stock exchange. A stock exchange is exactly as its name implies: It is a place where people who own stock or shares in a company go to buy or sell shares. There are a few different stock exchanges that a company can use, but the biggest is known as the New York Stock Exchange.

Now that you know what a share of stock is, you need to know a few rules about owning stock, especially within a 401(k) plan.

THE DIVERSIFICATION PRINCIPLE

A basic rule of investing is that you never want all your money to be invested in just one or two or even a handful of stocks. The reason is pretty simple: If you have 100 percent of your money invested in one stock, and that stock goes down, you are going to be in big trouble. What you want to do is own many different stocks that are in different types of industries or services. This is what is known as *diversification*. Which is why the majority of your money should be in the mutual funds of your 401(k) plan: Even if your plan offers you shares of your company's stock, you still should make mutual funds the centerpiece of your 401(k) fund. Loading up on your company stock will leave you undiversified.

WHAT IS A MUTUAL FUND?

A stock mutual fund is simply a fund that owns dozens, if not hundreds, of individual stocks. A mutual fund gives you instant diversification: You buy shares of a mutual fund, and each share gives you a stake in all the different stocks owned by the fund.

Another difference: You decide when to buy or sell a stock. With a mutual fund, a portfolio manager decides what stocks to buy and sell for the fund. You, of course, have control over whether you want to buy shares of the fund or sell your shares, but the portfolio manager controls the decision making about what investments to hold inside that fund.

So your big decision with your 401(k) is which funds to invest in.

HOW TO INVEST YOUR MONEY IN A 401(K)

You want your 401(k) to be invested in stock mutual funds. Your plan will probably also offer mutual funds such as bond funds and something called stable-value funds. Please don't invest in these options unless you are just a few years away from retirement. Let me tell you why.

The majority of you who still have at least ten years before retirement belong in individual stocks or stock mutual funds. When you invest for the long term in a retirement account, stocks or stock mutual funds offer you the best opportunity for gains to help you meet your retirement goals and give you the best chance of earning returns that are higher than the rate of inflation. Bonds and stable-value funds don't have as much upside potential as stocks. Now, that said, it is absolutely true that stocks have plenty of downside, too. Anyone who was invested in stocks from 2000 to 2003 knows exactly what I am talking about. But you need to grasp this central rule of investing: Over time—decades, not months—stocks outperform bonds and, yes, your savings account, too. The historical average annual rate is more than 10 percent for stocks, just half that for bonds, and even less for your savings accounts.

I realize that many of you are worried about investing in stocks; you view them as being too risky or volatile. Well, you should be just as concerned that if you keep your money in very conservative investments, such as bonds or cash (savings accounts), you run the risk that your money will not grow enough to support you in retirement. That's a risk you can't afford to take. Yes, stocks can be volatile from month to month and year to year. But when you are investing for a goal that is ten years or more away, you can ride out the downturns and have your money invested to take advantage of periods when stocks rally.

So now you know you need to focus on stock funds, but your plan has many to choose from and you have no clue which one to select.

This is what I want you to do: First, you have to decide if you want to make a move once and never look at your portfolio again. If the answer to that is yes, which essentially means you want to go on automatic pilot from today until the day you retire, this is what I want you to do:

Opt for a Lifecycle Fund

Chances are your plan offers this one-fund solution—what I call the One and Done option. To find out if you have one of these kinds of funds in your 401(k) plan, call your HR person or take a look at your options online or get in touch with customer service.

If there is a fund with the word "lifecycle" or "lifestyle" in it and you feel this is the way for you to go, all you have to do is choose the option in the lifecycle fund that has a retirement year (it will be part of the fund's name) that reflects when you expect to retire. Typically, you can choose funds with target retirement dates that are anywhere from five years to forty years away. The fund then automatically holds (and adjusts over time) the proper types of investments—according to investment pros—based on how many years you have until retirement. For example, if you pick a lifecycle/target fund with a retirement year forty years off, it will own mostly stocks right now; then, as you get closer to retirement, it will automatically scale back its investments in stocks and shift to less risky investments. The fund will also automatically "allocate" your investments in a wide range of types of stocks: stocks from different countries, stocks from different industries, small stocks, large stocks, and so on.

Opting for a lifecycle fund is fine, especially if you do not want to have to think about your money again, but I have to tell you they aren't my perfect solution. Many of these funds hold bonds or even some cash. That's not horrible, and there are some good reasons why they do this, but ideally, I think when you are twenty, thirty, or forty years away from retirement, you should really focus mostly on stock funds. If you are willing to pay just a little bit more attention to your money, then there is a better option that is practically as easy to put in place.

Opt for Index Funds

Take a look at your investing options again and search for any fund with the name "index" or "500" or "total market" or "extended market" in the name. These types of funds are index funds. Instead of being run by a manager or a team of money managers who are responsible for deciding what stocks the fund will own, an index fund removes the human element. You aren't investing in the ability of a money manager to be a market guru who makes great calls on what to own and what to sell; you are investing in a fund that simply aims to mimic the performance of a popular market benchmark. One of the most well-known market indexes is the Standard & Poor's 500. This index is made up of 500 different stocks of well-known companies—what are referred to as the "blue chips."

If your 401(k) plan offers an index fund that mirrors the S&P 500, that's a fine choice. But an even better option, in my opinion, is an index fund that tracks an even broader index. Funds that have "extended" or "total" in their name tend to track indexes of 4,500 or more stocks. Not 500, but 4,500. Instead of just blue chips, you own a broader array of different types of stocks—blue chips and smaller firms. A 500-index fund gives you very good diversification. An extended or total index gives you great diversification.

The bigger point here is that indexing, period, is a great way to go. The truth is that very few money managers who "actively run" mutual funds—meaning they get to pick and choose the stocks in their fund—have been able to do better than the benchmarks year after year. Relying on an index fund can often produce better returns over the years than relying on money managers.

If there's an index fund option, great. Mark it down. But you are not quite done yet. Next I want you to look for a fund in your plan that invests in international stocks. A little care is needed here. You may have an "international" option as well as an "emerging markets" option. The difference is that the emerging-markets funds invest in stocks in countries that are considered less "mature" or "developed." This can mean tremendous opportunity—China, for example, has been quite a successful emerging-market economy—but plenty of risk, too. While I think it is very important to have exposure—that is, to be invested in international stocks, given that we live in a global economy—I am not going to insist you take on emerging markets. An international fund primarily invests in foreign companies centered in countries that are considered more established. Some plans offer an international index fund; that's a great choice.

If you opt for either the lifecycle or index strategies for your 401(k), I will indeed be thrilled; you will be properly invested for retirement. But I want to be clear: These strategies are a great "minimum-effort" approach. As you can see from the menu of investing options in your plan, in addition to the basic lifecycle and index funds there are many different types of funds to invest in. Each of these funds has a different investment goal. Some funds focus on big, established companies that have been around for years (large-cap funds), while others invest only in smaller, younger firms that have the potential for big growth (small-cap funds). You will also find funds that use a specific investment strategy—a fund with the word "growth" in it tends to hold stocks of companies that are expected to have big jumps in their earnings. Other funds focus on stocks that have been a bit lackluster or beaten up lately but are expected to rebound; these are known as "value" stocks. Of course, the risk on all of these varies, so it's important to know what you are getting into and whether you can afford to take these risks.

On my website I have information on how to decipher the different types of mutual funds offered in your 401(k), as well as strategies for how and when it can make sense to add more funds to your 401(k) portfolio. I also have a tutorial that walks you through every line of your 401(k) statement.

Your 401(k) Allocation

▲ 90 percent in your index fund that follows a broad benchmark of U.S. stocks; look for index funds with "total stock" or "extended market" in the name.

▲ 10 percent in an international fund or international index fund.

You want all your new contributions to aim for this allocation mix. You can call the customer service department of the firm that handles your company's retirement plan or go online to their website to change how your current contributions are allocated. If you have been investing in your 401(k) for some time and have money already in other funds, you have complete freedom to move that money into index and international funds (assuming your plan offers them). There is no cost or tax penalty for doing this.

That's it. You are properly invested in your 401(k).

GETTING CLOSE TO RETIREMENT?

For those of you who are a few years away from retirement, my advice would be to begin to switch your money into the stable-value funds within your 401(k) plan. Not bond funds—bond funds go up and down in value depending on what is happening with interest rates. Stable-value funds have a goal to keep your value stable. A stable-value fund in fact invests in bonds, but it has an added component that aims to eliminate the ups and downs that come with changes in interest rates. It's a conservative-type bond fund that is structured so the value of your account won't drop; that is, it will be stable. The upside is the interest rate you earn on the investment; typically, it is going to be one or two percentage points more than what you can earn in a savings account or money market account.

The reason I suggest shifting some of your money from stock funds to stable-value funds is to reduce your risk. Remember, I recommend stocks and stock funds when you have at least ten years or more to keep the money invested, but if you are retiring and expect you will need that money in a few years, you want to add some protection to your account. If you stay 100 percent invested in stocks, you run the risk that your account will suffer a big loss if the stock market goes into one of its swoons just as you want to start withdrawing money. So what you want to do is start slowly moving some of your stock fund money into stable-value funds. This reduces the overall volatility of your account.

But don't automatically move everything into stable value when you are fifty-five or sixty. It's important to keep some of your money invested in stocks, because the reality is that you are just fifty-five or sixty years young! The odds are that many of you could live another twenty years or more. So what you want to do is just move a portion of your money out of stock funds and into stable value. You need both the stability that stable-value funds provide and the earnings potential of stocks. My general advice is:

- ▲ By the time you are sixty, you might want to have 35 percent or so of your money in stable-value funds.
- ▲ Between sixty and seventy, you might want to increase that to 50 percent.
- ▲ After seventy, you can shift another 5 percent into stable value each year, so that . . .
- ▲ By the time you are eighty, you are not invested in stocks or stock funds.

That is just a general strategy. What makes sense for you depends on your individual situation. For example, if you expect to leave your 401(k) to your heirs—that is, you won't need to use the money to support yourself in retirement—then you don't need to lower your risk aggressively. You can leave the money in stock and stock funds so it grows for future generations. The only reason to switch to more conservative investments as you age is to lower your risk that the portfolio will have a sharp decrease in value just at the point when you will depend on that money to pay for your living expenses in retirement.

ABOUT THAT COMPANY STOCK ...

As I said earlier, some retirement plans allow you to invest in your company's own stock. In fact, some plans insist that the matching employer contribution be invested in company stock.

If your plan offers company stock, you need to be very careful. Remember that diversification talk we had a few minutes ago? Well, if your 401(k) is 50 percent invested in your own company's stock, you are not diversified.

I recommend that your company's own stock not amount to more than 10 percent of your total invested assets. Not just your 401(k) assets, but your total invested assets. That's how you protect yourself from any nasty surprises. It brings to mind the Enron disaster. So many of Enron's employees had their entire 401(k) invested solely in Enron stock. Those people didn't just lose their jobs when Enron went bankrupt; their entire retirement accounts were wiped out, because they were full of Enron stock.

Granted, a company the size of Enron going under is rare, but you need to be realistic about all sorts of risks: that your company's stock could suffer if a competitor gains ground; that the entire industry could fall out of favor; or that economic turmoil halfway around the globe could hurt your company's growth prospects. The point is that you can't know for sure that any single company is always going to be a good investment, all the time.

Keep your company stock to 10 percent or less of your total assets. If your company previously tied your hands by giving you the company stock as your matching contribution, check back with HR. Because of Enron and other problems, there are now new rules in place that encourage employers to make it easier for employees to move their money out of the company stock and into other funds offered in the plan.

LEAVE YOUR MONEY ALONE!

I cannot say this clearly or strongly enough: Do not touch your money before you reach retirement age. Here are two crippling mistakes I see so many people make, and it puts their retirement years on shaky ground.

No Loans

Many 401(k) plans allow you to take a loan from your account. Basically, you are allowed to raid your retirement kitty with the understanding that you will pay yourself back—with interest—within five years. Under no circumstances is this ever a good idea:

▲ If you are laid off or decide to take a new job, you typically need to repay whatever amount of the loan is still outstanding within a few months. If you don't come up with the cash to repay the loan, you will owe a 10 percent penalty (assuming you are under fifty-five in the year you left the job) as well as income tax on the money you withdrew from the account.

▲ You will end up paying tax twice on the money you withdrew. When you invest in your regular 401(k), you use pretax dollars—that is, money that has yet to be taxed. But when you take that money out as a loan, the dollars you use to pay back the loan will come from money that has already been taxed. Then, when you go to take the money out again later on when you are actually retired—guess what? You will pay tax again on that money; remember—all money withdrawn from a 401(k) is taxed at your ordinary income tax rate. The IRS just loves people who take out loans from their 401(k) plans; these people volunteer to pay taxes on that money twice.

No Cash-Outs

When you leave a company—voluntarily or not—you no longer have to stay invested in that company's 401(k). You have four different options: keep the money in that plan as long as you have at least $5,000 or more; move the money into your new employer's plan; move the money into what is known as an IRA rollover account; or take the money in cash. You are never—and I mean *never*—to take that fourth option. I don't care if you have just $1,500 in your 401(k) and really need that money. Remember: If you need it now, you will most likely need it even more when you get older.

First, as a general rule, you will owe a 10 percent penalty—as well as income tax—on money you withdraw from your 401(k) before age 59½. One important exception: If you are fifty-five or older in the year you retired, took another job, or were laid off, you can withdraw any amount of money you want from your 401(k) without having to pay the 10 percent penalty. This is not true for traditional IRAs or IRA rollovers, just for retirement accounts like a 401(k).

Okay, let's say you don't listen to me and you withdraw the $1,500 you have in your 401(k) account. You are forty years of age and you think you really need it right now and it really isn't that much money. Because you are still young you will owe a 10 percent penalty on that money and you will owe income tax on the withdrawn amount. Let's assume you are in the 25 percent federal tax bracket. After paying the penalty and income tax, you will have about $1,000 left over that you will spend on something that you will not even remember in a few years.

Now let's consider what happens if instead you listen to me, leave the $1,500 invested for retirement, and earn an 8 percent annualized rate of return. After ten years, that $1,500 will be worth $3,200. Over twenty years, it grows to nearly $7,000. After thirty years, it is worth more than $15,000. So don't tell me that it's "only" $1,500. It's a lot more than that.

When you leave a job, knowing what to do with your 401(k) can indeed be confusing. On my website I explain all your options in detail, including my favorite: moving your 401(k) money into either an IRA rollover at a discount brokerage or mutual fund company. With an IRA rollover, you still get all the tax advantages of your 401(k), but you expand your investing options beyond the funds offered in your former employer's plan.

ROTH 401(K)S: THE NEW KID ON THE BLOCK

Beginning in 2006, employers were permitted to expand their 401(k) to offer what is known as a Roth 401(k). So far, not many companies have added a Roth version to their 401(k) plans, but I expect that to change in the coming years. If your company offers a Roth 401(k), consider yourself lucky. In my opinion, it is a better deal than a regular 401(k) for almost everyone.

The big difference between a regular 401(k) and a Roth 401(k) is how you are taxed. With a Roth 401(k), you will get no up-front tax break: The money you contribute into the plan is money that has already been taxed. But the potential big break comes when you retire and start withdrawing money from the plan. With a Roth 401(k), if you meet some basic rules, all your withdrawals will be tax-free, whereas withdrawals from a traditional 401(k) will be fully taxed at whatever your income tax rate is in retirement. Typically, the younger you are, the more sense a Roth 401(k) makes.

▲ **Information on how Roth 401(k)s work, and when they make more sense than traditional 401(k)s, is available on my website.**

RETIREMENT SAVING ON YOUR OWN

A 401(k) with an employer match is a great core investment for building retirement security, but not all companies offer it, and in truth, even if you do have a plan at work, you also need to do some additional retirement saving on your own. It's important to do everything possible today—*save* everything possible—to build the biggest retirement nest egg you can. So whether you have a 401(k) you are funding up to the company match, or if you do not have such a plan through work, you should have additional retirement accounts that you set up, invest in, and manage *on your own*.

Take Advantage of a Roth IRA

There is one special type of retirement account that I want everyone who qualifies to have, and that is a Roth Individual Retirement Account. Yes, I want you to participate in a 401(k) because of the great "bonus" of the employer match, but I believe that after the point of the match (or if your company does not match at all) the Roth is actually a better deal.

First, you need to know that you can have both a 401(k) and a Roth. That said, not everyone is eligible for a Roth IRA; as I will explain, there are certain income limits. That doesn't mean you can't save for retirement on your own. In fact, Congress slid through a quirky new rule recently that creates a great opportunity for anyone who currently can't invest in a Roth. It's an amazing financial move that I am using myself, but I will get to that in a bit. First things first.

Too many advisors to this day still do not understand how Roths work, and so you are missing out. Now, pay close attention to what I have to say about Roth IRAs and consider it law. But in order to appreciate how great a Roth is, you first have to understand its predecessor, the traditional IRA.

TRADITIONAL IRAS

More than thirty years ago, Congress recognized that it needed to come up with an incentive for people to save for retirement on their own. So they created the individual retirement account (IRA). Anyone with earned income (and earned income is simply income that you yourself earned, not interest income or rental income) can set up an IRA and, depending on their income, deduct the contributions from their taxable income.

The rules on who is allowed to deduct IRA contributions on their federal tax return are as follows:

▲ If you are single and do not have a retirement plan at work, you can invest in an IRA and deduct your contributions regardless of your income (the adjusted gross income, AGI, you report on your tax return).

▲ If you are single and have a retirement plan at work, you can deduct your IRA contribution if your AGI is below $60,000.

▲ If you are married, file a joint tax return, and *neither* of you has a retirement plan through your employer, you both can invest in an IRA and deduct your contributions regardless of your AGI.

▲ If you are married, file a joint tax return, and you both contribute to a retirement plan through work, you will be allowed to deduct your IRA contributions only if your joint AGI is below $100,000.

▲ If you are married, file a joint tax return, and do not actively participate in a retirement plan through work but your spouse does, you can make a deductible IRA contribution if your joint AGI is below $160,000.

(Note: If your income falls into certain phase-out ranges set by the IRS, the amount you can invest in a deductible IRA will be limited. The phase-out affects singles with income between $50,000 and $60,000 and married couples filing a joint tax return with income between $150,000 and $160,000.)

Even if you can't deduct the contribution from your tax bill, anyone can open a nondeductible IRA: Though there's no initial tax break, you get all the other benefits of tax-deferred investing. While the money stays in the account, you can invest in almost anything you want and all the growth of that money over all the years you remain invested is not taxed. That way, money you normally would be paying taxes on sits in this IRA making money for you, not the IRS. Only when you withdraw the money do you owe income tax—on the amount withdrawn.

ROTH IRA

In 1998, a new type of IRA hit the market. The Roth IRA, named in honor of its champion, Senator William Roth, takes a different approach than a traditional IRA. You fund a Roth IRA with money you have already paid taxes on. Because you invested after-tax money, if you abide by just a few simple rules, all the money you invest and all of the growth on that money will be tax-free when you take it out. That's quite different from a traditional IRA; different, too, from a 401(k). With both those types of investments, you owe income tax on whatever money you withdraw.

Penalty and Tax-Free Withdrawals Anytime You Want

Here is the other great feature of a Roth: If you suddenly need money from your Roth IRA, you can withdraw any of your contributions without any tax or penalty—regardless of your age or how long the money has been in there. With a traditional IRA or a 401(k), you typically owe income tax and a 10 percent penalty on any money you withdraw before age 59½. Big difference. Let me give you an example of the wonderful flexibility a Roth offers.

Let's say you are thirty-five years old and invest $4,000 in a Roth IRA this year, $4,000 next year, and $4,000 the following year. You have invested a total of $12,000. Now let's say that the $12,000 you invested has grown in value, so your account is worth $13,000. If you wanted, you could withdraw up to $12,000 (the amount you have contributed to the Roth) for any need, without any penalty or tax, even though you are now just thirty-eight years old and the account has been open only three years. In this example, it is just the $1,000 in earnings that you need to leave in the Roth until you are 59½ to avoid taxes and penalties.

Now, I am not advocating treating your Roth IRA as a vacation fund; I just want you to understand that in an actual emergency you have access to your contributions without tax or penalty. With a Roth, you really don't have to worry about your money being "locked up."

Not So Fast—You Still Need a Separate Emergency Savings Account

Now, I know what you might be thinking: *Great, I don't need to invest in a savings account. I can just put money in a Roth IRA and use it for emergencies.* No, no, no. This is not a smart move. You want to have an emergency savings fund—what we discussed in Month One—as well as a Roth IRA. I only wanted you to understand that as a last resort, your Roth IRA can be a backup emergency account. Pay attention to the key words I used: "last resort" and "backup."

If you can fully fund both the savings account and the Roth

IRA, great. If money is tight, just be strategic: Take whatever you have to invest each month and divide it between your two goals. For example, if you have a total of $200 you can invest each month, put $100 in the savings account and $100 in your Roth IRA.

I ♥ Roths

Here is another advantage of a Roth, especially for women. Let's say that when you reach retirement you would like to pay off your home mortgage. Nothing would make you feel more secure. When you reach 59½, assuming you have had the account for at least five years, you can withdraw 100 percent of your money without paying any tax and use it to pay off your mortgage or pay down any other debt you might have. In fact, it's all yours for whatever purpose. What you see in your account is what ends up in your wallet, yours to spend as you wish. Remember, in a 401(k) or traditional IRA, whatever money you take out will be taxed as ordinary income at whatever income-tax rates are in place at that time. If you take out $200,000, you will be lucky if you have $150,000 left after taxes. What you see is definitely not what you get.

A Roth also gives you more choice about what you can do with your money in retirement. With a Roth, you are not required to make any withdrawals if you don't need the money. With IRAs and 401(k)s, you are essentially forced to start taking money out once you reach the age of 70½. That can make a big difference for your heirs; you can leave more money in your Roth for your loved ones to inherit. And any money that is left in your Roth upon your death will pass tax-free to whomever you have designated as your beneficiary. With a 401(k) or traditional IRA, your heirs will need to pay ordinary income taxes on the money they inherit and withdraw.

So now you can see why I want every woman who is eligible for a Roth IRA to start investing in one right now. If you qualify for a Roth, you cannot afford to pass it up. Do you hear me?

Qualifying for a Roth

As of 2007, you qualify for a Roth IRA if:

▲ You are single and your modified adjusted gross income (MAGI) is below $114,000.
▲ You are married and file a joint tax return, with MAGI below $166,000.

Are you wondering what "modified adjusted gross income" means? Listen, if you are not even close to making that kind of money—let's say you are single and you make $50,000 a year—don't worry about MAGI; you are fine. For those of you whose income is near those limits, here is what I want you to do to see if you qualify for a Roth. Pull out your federal tax return from last year. If you filed Form 1040, check what you reported on line 38 as your adjusted gross income (AGI). For most of you, your AGI is going to be close to your MAGI, so let's just use that for now as our guide to determining your eligibility.

Roth Annual Contribution Limits

The maximum amount you can invest in a Roth IRA in 2007 is $4,000 if you are under fifty years old and $5,000 if you are fifty or older. In 2008, the limit will be $5,000 if you are under fifty and $6,000 if you are over fifty. The annual limits will be adjusted in line with inflation for subsequent years.

A SPECIAL NOTE TO STAY-AT-HOME MOMS AND NONWORKING SPOUSES

Just because you don't earn a paycheck doesn't mean you can't have a Roth. You can have a spousal IRA, be it a Roth or a traditional IRA. The money you invest in the IRA can come from the income your spouse earns, but what I especially like is that the actual account will be in your name only—not in your spouse's name, not held as a joint account. That's a nice power move. In reality, if you were ever to divorce, money acquired and invested during a marriage is going to have to be equitably distributed. And in community property states, it typically is an automatic 50-50 split. But having the account in your name puts some control and responsibility in your lap—and your lap only. Again, your goal is to have both a savings account and your spousal IRA account; I recommend working on funding both at the same time. So take whatever money you have each month and divide it between the two goals: Half goes toward building your emergency savings account and half goes toward your spousal IRA.

INVEST AT YOUR OWN PACE

There are two methods you can use to invest in a Roth or traditional IRA.

You can make one large investment one time a year, or you can choose to invest a smaller amount each month or each quarter. Investing all at once is called lump-sum investing. So if you have $4,000 or $5,000, you can put it into your Roth all at once, in one lump sum. Pretty basic.

But if you don't have $4,000 or $5,000 handy at one time, you can use the "periodic" approach to investing in your Roth

IRA—a method known as **dollar cost averaging**. For example, to end up with $4,000 invested over the course of a year, you could invest $333 a month. While I would love for you to invest that much, I want you to understand that you can invest less than $4,000, too, if you simply do not have the money.

If $50 a month is what works in your budget today, that's fine. Please don't talk yourself out of saving for retirement because you don't think $50 a month is going to make a difference. I know we covered this in the first month of the plan, but I want to reemphasize the point: A little adds up to a lot over time.

Invest $50 a month and earn an 8 percent annualized rate on your investment and you will have:
$9,208 in 10 years
$29,647 in 20 years
$75,015 in 30 years
$175,714 in 40 years

You can see how your monthly investment will grow over time with my Dollar Cost Averaging Calculator on my website.

HOW TO CHOOSE THE RIGHT INVESTMENT FOR YOUR IRA OR ROTH

If you simply send in a check to a brokerage or mutual fund company to open an IRA or a Roth account without making it clear what you want your money invested in, chances are your money will just sit in a savings account or money market account, and that's the absolute worst thing you can do. Remember, if you have at least ten years or more until you retire, you need to invest in the stock market to get the best returns on your money over the long haul.

Smart Investments for Lump-Sum Investors

If you intend to invest in your IRA or Roth just once a year, the first thing you need to know is that the best time to do so is in January. That way, your money is working in an advantageous way all year long, which can amount to a lot of money over time.

When it's time to invest, I happen to think exchange-traded funds (ETFs) are a great choice. An ETF is very similar to an index fund; it, too, aims to mimic the performance of a benchmark index, just like a regular index mutual fund.

In fact, you can often find an ETF and an index mutual fund that are tracking the same exact benchmark. They just have a few small differences; think of them more as fraternal twins rather than identical twins:

▲ An ETF trades like a stock on a stock exchange. That means during the day you can buy and sell shares of your ETF and your price is whatever the ETF was trading at when your order was placed. A mutual fund is a bit different. Mutual funds don't trade during the day; their price is set just once a day *after* the market closes, which is at 4 P.M. EDT Monday to Friday. So let's say you decide to buy or sell your fund shares at 11 A.M. You go online or call customer service and place your order at 11 A.M. The actual price you will get on your mutual fund trade will be based on the closing value of all the stocks in the portfolio. So you essentially have to wait until the mutual fund sets its price after the 4 P.M. close to know what price you will get.

In market-ese, an ETF is thought to offer more liquidity than a mutual fund. An ETF's price changes throughout the trading day based on what is happening to the underlying stocks it owns. This liquidity issue is a big deal for day traders, people who aggressively buy and sell stocks throughout the day; with an ETF, they can jump on changes in stock values during the trading day. But that's not what your retirement investing is all about; you are investing for the long term and aren't going to be constantly trading your account.

So why am I recommending ETFs? That brings us to the second difference between index mutual funds and ETFs:

▲ An ETF can cost you less in annual fees. A good ETF will often have a lower expense ratio than a mutual fund. Let's slow down for a second and talk about expense ratios.

Expense ratio: An expense ratio is an annual fee that both ETFs and mutual funds charge to cover their management and administrative costs. Everyone pays this fee—it is actually shaved off the fund's performance each year; it is not a separate line item you will see deducted on your statement. Obviously, the lower your expense ratio the better.

While the expense ratio on index mutual funds tends to be low, it can be even lower for an ETF. That's why I like ETFs for your IRA. The less you pay in fees, the more money you have left to grow for your future.

However, ETFs don't make sense if you are going to make periodic investments (dollar cost averaging) on a monthly or even quarterly basis. The reason is that ETFs have to be bought just like a stock—that is, you must pay a commission every time you buy or sell shares of an ETF. At the discount brokerage TD Ameritrade, the commission for each trade is $9.99. That's a terrific deal. But if you invest monthly and end up paying that $9.99 every month, you will end up spending about $120 a year in commissions. If you invest $333 a month, or $4,000 over the course of the year, in your Roth, that $120 commission works out to a 3 percent sales fee. That's not a good use of your money. That's why I only recommend ETFs for lump-sum investors. For someone who could invest $4,000 in one lump sum, the cost to invest all that money in one ETF would be $9.99.

When you invest, follow the same straightforward strategy we used for your 401(k) choices:

▲ 90 percent of your money in an ETF that tracks a broad U.S. benchmark
▲ 10 percent in a diversified international fund

One good, low-cost ETF that tracks a broad U.S. index is the **Vanguard Extended Market** (ticker symbol VTI). A low-cost ETF that invests in international stocks that I like is the **iShares MSCI EAFE** index ETF (ticker symbol EFA).

Where and How to Open an ETF Account

If you intend to be a lump-sum investor, I encourage you to consider opening your IRA account at a discount brokerage firm. The "discount" in discount brokerage means that you are charged lower fees when you buy and sell investments than you would be at a full-service brokerage that provides additional hand-holding support, research, and a bunch of other services that you probably don't need. All the hand-holding you need to invest your IRA properly is right here in this book.

On the websites, look for the links for retirement or IRA investing. To open an account, you will need to download a form, fill it out, and send it back in. In addition to the usual personal information, your IRA investment form will ask you to choose what investments you want your IRA to be invested in and how you intend to send in your money. You can do a direct electronic transfer from your savings or money market account to the brokerage—the form you fill out will tell you what information you need to provide—or you can simply send in an old-fashioned check. It is a very straightforward process, but I know it can still feel a bit scary the first time you go through it. Keep in mind that financial firms are dying to get you to invest at their firm. So if you start getting confused or lost, contact customer service. They will be very motivated to help you get your money invested with them.

For a list of the best discount brokerages, go to my website.

Smart Roth and IRA Investments for the Investor Contributing Small Amounts over the Course of a Year

If you plan to put money into your Roth or IRA account every month or so, you should invest in no-load mutual funds. A load is a fee—a commission or sales charge. Therefore, a no-load is a no-commission fund. I always want you to use no-load funds. There's no reason you should pay anything to buy a mutual fund. That said, I want to make sure you understand that a load is not the same as the expense ratio I mentioned earlier. The expense ratio is a completely separate charge that all mutual funds (and all ETFs) have; it is an annual charge everyone pays. The object is to choose mutual funds that have no load and have the smallest possible annual expense ratio.

How Are Loads Charged?

Loads can be charged in two basic ways: up front when you first invest, or as a deferred sales charge that you may have to pay when you sell your shares.

A Share Funds: Funds that charge a load when you invest have an A following their name. They are often called A share funds. An average A share load is 5 percent or so. So if you invest $4,000, only $3,800 will actually be invested in your account. The other $200 (5 percent) goes to pay the broker or financial advisor who sold you the fund. That's their commission. Just think about that: You start out 5 percent in the hole. You need your fund to gain back the $200 for you just to break even.

And it's not as if an A share fund guarantees you great performance. The load you pay has nothing to do with the talent of the fund manager (and if you are investing in an index fund, there's actually no talent needed). The load simply pays the person who sold you the fund.

B Share Funds: Funds that can charge you a commission when you sell have a B at the end of their name. They are called B share funds. They look great because you don't pay a commission when you invest. You will, however, pay a fee if you leave within a few years. Typically, you can get hit with a 5 percent sales charge if you sell within the first year, 4 percent within two years, and so on. On top of that, the expense ratio on a deferred-load fund is a lot higher than the expense ratio on a true no-load fund, especially a low-cost index fund. I think all B share funds should be avoided like the plague. If you see the letter B after the name of the mutual fund, don't buy it!

How to Spot a Load Fund

As I note above, the easiest way to spot a load fund is seeing if there's an A or B after the name of the fund. But here is another way: Before you invest in any fund, you can look it up at the fund company's website or call up customer service and ask about the fees. Here's what you want to know:

▲ Do I pay a load when I buy shares of this fund?
▲ Will I pay a load if I sell my shares within, say, five years? (That's the B share tip-off.)

If the answer to either question is yes, you are looking at a loaded fund.

To learn more about mutual funds, go to www.morningstar. com. At the top of the page, you can enter the name or ticker symbol for a mutual fund, and it will take you to a data page for that fund. (The ticker symbol is an abbreviation for an investment. A mutual fund ticker symbol always has five letters and ends in X.) On the right side of the page, you will clearly see information about the expense ratio as well as any loads.

The same investing strategy we used with your 401(k) works with your no-load funds:

▲ 90 percent in a no-load mutual fund that tracks a broad market benchmark
▲ 10 percent in a no-load mutual fund that invests in international stocks from developed countries

Where and How to Open a No-Load-Fund Roth or IRA

The T. Rowe Price mutual fund group is a great place to open a Roth IRA (www.troweprice.com; 800-638-5660). You can open an account where you invest as little as $50 a month. T. Rowe's Extended Equity Market Index fund is a smart choice for your core index fund; they also have an international stock fund for the remaining 10 percent of your Roth strategy.

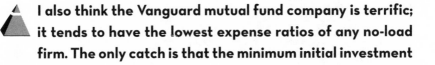 **I also think the Vanguard mutual fund company is terrific; it tends to have the lowest expense ratios of any no-load firm. The only catch is that the minimum initial investment**

for its funds is $3,000 (and then $100 after that). On my website I lay out a strategy for how to build a Roth IRA using Vanguard funds.

KEEP ALL YOUR IRAS IN ONE PLACE

Whether you choose to invest in ETFs or mutual funds, I strongly urge you to keep your IRA investment with one firm. That's because many discount brokerages and fund firms will charge you an annual maintenance fee—they call it a custodial fee—for each separate IRA. The account custodial fee can be $10 to $50 or more. Often once your account reaches a certain level—say, $10,000 or more—the fee may be waived. If you already have two or three IRAs at different brokerages, please check your statement and see how much you are paying in a custodial fee on each account. Move all your accounts to the firm with the best investing options and lowest fees. By consolidating your various accounts into one account, you may have enough money to get the custodial fee waived.

How to Transfer IRA Money

You will need to fill out some forms from both the firm that currently holds your IRA and the firm you want to move your money to. If you already have an account at the firm you want to move your money to, then all you need to do is complete the form to add to your existing account. If you do not currently have an account at that firm, then you want to open a new IRA account. In both instances, in the paperwork there will be an option for "asset transfer"; that is, you will be transferring money from an existing IRA into your new account. That's what you choose. And be very careful here: You want this transfer to be done without your touching the money. You are not to get a check from the old firm for the value of your IRA and then be responsible for investing that money in your new IRA. This triggers a bunch of IRS/tax problems. Listen to me: Just check the "asset transfer" option.

The fund firm or brokerage will ask you some questions about the account you want moved, such as the name on the account, the account number, and so on. This will allow the firm to go to your existing IRA firm and request that the money be transferred. But before that can happen, you may need to fill out another form with the firm you are leaving, authorizing them to transfer the money. Basically, your job is to sign the paperwork so the two financial firms can work with each other without your involvement. In most instances, the firm you are moving money into will require that the form you sign include a "signature guarantee." What this means is that you take the (unsigned) transfer form and your driver's license or other photo ID down to your bank and for free your bank will put an official stamp on it. It's just a fancy version of getting your signature notarized.

IRA INVESTING IF YOU DON'T QUALIFY FOR A ROTH

Even if you make too much money to qualify for a Roth IRA, you still need to have your own retirement fund outside of a company plan. A fabulous gift bestowed by Congress in 2006 has created a backdoor way for people with high incomes to invest in a Roth.

First, I want to review a few things about traditional IRAs: There are certain rules you have to meet to be able to deduct your contribution, but no matter how high your income is, or whether or not you also have a retirement account at work, anyone can invest in a **nondeductible** traditional IRA. All the same rules apply as with other traditional IRA investments: same contribution limits, same deferred tax treatment while your money is invested. You just aren't able to deduct your initial contribution on your federal tax bill.

Now, here's where it gets interesting: In 2006, Congress passed a law that will allow high-income individuals with traditional IRAs to convert to a Roth IRA beginning in 2010. So you can't open a Roth directly today, but if you open a traditional IRA, Congress is going to let you change it into a Roth IRA beginning in 2010. The conversion will be allowed for everyone, regardless of how much you make.

THIS IS MAJOR NEWS!
As of 2010, everyone will be able to have a Roth as part of their retirement planning.

Now, here is what I want you to do if you do not qualify for a Roth IRA:

Fund a Traditional IRA Today and Convert to a Roth in 2010

This is your game plan: Invest in a traditional IRA today and keep funding it to the max. Then, beginning in 2010, you can convert the money into a Roth IRA. You do not have to convert 100 percent of the account; you can choose any amount you want. To do this, you will contact the brokerage firm or fund firm where you have your traditional IRA and fill out a conversion form. (You will also be able to convert any money you may have already invested in a traditional IRA from years past.) The downside is that when you convert, you will owe tax. If you are converting a deductible IRA, you will owe tax on the entire amount of the conversion. If your traditional IRA was nondeductible, you will owe tax only on what you have earned; your original contributions are not taxed, because after all, they were made with money you already paid taxes on.

▲ **If you have both deductible and nondeductible IRAs, the IRS has some maddening rules on what tax you will pay on a Roth conversion. Go to my website for help navigating these very tricky waters.**

But don't let this dissuade you. That tax hit today means you will never ever owe a penny of tax on that money again! Remember, once your money is in a Roth, all withdrawals are tax-free, assuming you follow some basic rules. You pay tax today so you won't have to pay tax in retirement when you start to use the money.

An example will help illustrate what I'm talking about: Let's say you invest $4,000 in a traditional, nondeductible IRA in 2007, 2008, 2009, and 2010. So you have put in a total of $16,000. And let's say that $16,000 is worth $18,000 in 2010, thanks to the investment gains on your original contributions. If you convert that $18,000 into a Roth IRA, you will trigger an immediate tax bill on just the $2,000 gain. You don't owe tax on the $16,000 you invested, because that money came from your after-tax income. If you invested in a deductible IRA, you would owe tax on the entire amount converted, not just the gain.

When your money is converted to the Roth, your fund company or brokerage firm will report the change to the IRS. And that means the IRS is going to expect to hear from you: When you file your tax return, you will need to report the conversion and pay any tax you owe. (You report all this on IRS Form 8606.)

If you can handle paying the tax bill on a conversion—and you should make it a priority—it makes tremendous sense to invest in a traditional IRA with the intention of converting the money to a Roth IRA beginning in 2010. And unless Congress changes the law, you can continue to invest in traditional IRAs after 2010 and convert the money to a Roth IRA. Yes, you heard that right—even after 2010, you'll first have to fund a traditional IRA and then automatically convert it to a Roth. That's the way it is until lawmakers address this crazy dance. The bottom line is that, barring a change in federal law, you have an amazing opportunity to get your retirement money into a Roth through a back-door conversion.

▲ **The complete rules for converting a traditional IRA to a Roth IRA are covered on my website.**

So if you don't already contribute to a nondeductible IRA, you are to start right now. You can follow the same investing advice I already laid out in this month's plan.

JUGGLING YOUR 401(K) AND ROTH/IRA CONTRIBUTIONS

If money is tight and you can't easily fund your 401(k) and a Roth to their annual maximums—and I recognize that's a very tall order—you need to get strategic. Here's what I recommend:

▲ Make sure you contribute enough to your 401(k) to get the maximum annual matching contribution, but don't contribute a penny more than what you need to get that match. Your HR rep should be able to help you set your contribution at the correct level. This way you should have enough left over in your paycheck to work on investing in a Roth or IRA, too.
▲ If you don't get a company match in your 401(k) plan, make an IRA your first priority.
▲ Fund an IRA to the max, if you can.
▲ If you finish funding the IRA completely before year end and . . .
   . . . you are still building your emergency savings fund: Spend the rest of the year adding to your savings fund. When the new year rolls around, go back to focusing on funding your IRA again. (And, of course, you want to make sure you

will once again contribute enough to your 401(k) to get the maximum employer matching contribution.)

. . . you have finished building your emergency savings fund: Turn your focus back to your 401(k) and boost your contribution level for the rest of the year. Then, before the new year, you can reset your 401(k) contribution level back to what you need to get only the max match; that will leave more money in your paycheck, so you can once again make sure that you contribute to your IRA for the new year. Changing your contribution level on your 401(k) will take a call to HR or the plan administrator (the customer service department of the outside firm that handles your company's plan). And be sure to check ahead of time what the deadlines are for alerting the plan you want to change. Some plans make these changes just quarterly.

I realize that one of the biggest challenges in taking control of your financial life is figuring out your priorities. On my website I have specific strategies for how to organize and prioritize what you need to do. I tell you exactly how to juggle investing, saving, and debt payment, too.

A SPECIAL NOTE FOR WOMEN OVER FORTY-FIVE

If you live in the home you intend to retire in and it still has a mortgage, I want you to consider a different strategy. I always want you to invest in your 401(k) if you get a company match, but after you achieve that, I think it can be incredibly wise to forgo investing any more in retirement accounts and shift your attention—and money—to paying off your mortgage so you own your home outright by the time you retire.

For those of you who are at least forty-five years old and are living in a home you expect to retire in, I think it makes tremendous financial (and emotional) sense to try to pay off your mortgage ahead of schedule. Own your home free and clear before you retire and you have removed one of your biggest financial worries. Go to my website for strategies on how to own your home outright before retirement.

ACTION PLAN: SUMMARY FOR RETIREMENT INVESTING

✔ If your employer offers a 401(k) with a company match, make sure you participate in your plan and invest enough to get the maximum retirement bonus.

✔ Do not let company stock account for more than 10 percent of your investment assets.

✔ If you are at least ten years away from retirement, focus on stock mutual funds for your 401(k).

✔ Invest in a Roth IRA if you meet the income-eligibility rules.

✔ Invest in a traditional IRA if your income is too high to qualify for a Roth IRA, and plan to start converting your traditional IRA to a Roth IRA beginning in 2010.

✔ If you are a stay-at-home mom, invest in a spousal IRA.

✔ Invest just enough in your 401(k) to qualify for the maximum company match, while also funding an IRA to the annual maximum.

✔ Opt for ETFs for your IRA if you will be making one annual lump-sum investment.

✔ Opt for no-load mutual funds if you will be making smaller monthly or quarterly investments.

MONTH FOUR:
Must-Have Documents

Over the next two months, we are going to focus on making
sure you and your family are prepared for the major what-ifs of
life. The promise of this book—owning the power to control
your destiny—obviously cannot extend to life-changing events

beyond our control, such as illness, death, and natural disasters. However, we can prepare for certain eventualities—tough as they may be to face. All it requires is a little clearheaded thinking and the courage to have a few difficult conversations with our loved ones—and ourselves. As always, I will try my best to make the whole process as painless as possible.

Before we begin, I'm going to ask you to answer yes or no to a few very important questions. Please answer honestly.

▲ If you were to become gravely ill and could not speak for yourself, do you have the paperwork in place that would allow the person of your choosing to make urgent decisions regarding your health and medical care?

▲ If you were to become incapacitated, do you have the paperwork in place that would allow the person of your choosing to sign your checks and handle your financial affairs?

▲ If you were in a hospital on life support, do you have the paperwork in place that would allow the person of your choosing to communicate your wishes to the doctor?

▲ What if you died tomorrow? Are your dependent children protected? Do you have everything in place so that the adult of your choosing will handle the financial aspects of their care in the manner you wish?

▲ Do you have in place right here and now a revocable living trust so your assets will easily pass to your heirs without any cost or time delay? If so, does your trust have an incapacity clause in it?

If you answered yes to all of these questions, congratulations. I am thrilled. However, I still want you to read this entire chapter, because it is important to be sure that these documents contain everything necessary to make them completely effective. Having a document that is not correct can do even more damage than not having one at all.

If you answered no to any of these questions—and I'm feeling pretty confident that you did—this month's plan deserves your serious attention. If you answered no to all of them, let's say this together one more time: no shame, no blame.

The goal of this month's plan is to make sure that you have the paperwork in place to protect you and your family and make certain that your affairs are handled according to your wishes in the event of a tragedy. We are going to cover the specific legal documents you must have in place to set up your estate so your assets will be disbursed exactly as you want when you pass, and with maximum ease for your heirs. This is necessary for single women, for married women, for women with children and women without, for women with a good deal of money and women who are struggling to keep it together. **Every woman needs to pay attention here.**

Let's start our must-have-document discussion with a critically important fact:

WOMEN OUTLIVE MEN

We have all seen the statistics that show that women on average live longer than men. So those of you who are married stand a really good chance of spending your last years on this earth without your male counterpart. My own dad died in 1981 when my mom was just sixty-six. She is now ninety-one and has been on her own for more than a quarter century. Now, if we continue to use my family as an example, it means that at the age of fifty-five, and in fact for some time now, I take care of my mother's affairs and tend to her financial needs as well as my own. Without a doubt, I am blessed to have my mother with me all these years and blessed, too, that I can provide her with a comfortable life. But the statistical and actuarial reality is that we must consider the very real possibility that we could well have our children, ourselves, and our parents to look after all at once. Add to this the possibility that you might one day be the sole caretaker—if your husband passes before you—and you'll understand why I think it's more important than ever for you—*and your parents*—to have your documents in order.

Now, the fact that we tend to live longer means we have to deal with our money not only when we are sixty or seventy, but when we are eighty, ninety, and even one hundred. As we age, many of us may find it increasingly difficult to take care of every-day tasks, such as paying the bills or managing our money. We all hope that we and those we love will be able to evade Alzheimer's and dementia, but again, the goal this month is to anticipate the worst-case scenarios beyond our control and exert some control over them—to the extent that we are able, through planning and forethought, when we are strong and healthy.

THE MUST-HAVE DOCUMENTS

No matter who you are and what you have in this life, every single one of you needs the following three documents:

- ▲ A will
- ▲ A revocable living trust with an incapacity clause
- ▲ An advance directive and durable power of attorney for health care

WHY A WILL IS NOT ENOUGH

If you have any document in place, my guess is that it is a will. If this is the case, then I want you to know: **A will is not enough!** That's not to say wills are useless; they are, in fact, quite valuable. A will is where you indicate how you want certain assets and possessions to be passed on to your loved ones after your death.

A will states who is to inherit what upon your death. This is especially important if you are a mother of more than one child. A will can preempt any disputes among your heirs.

A will can also stipulate who will become the legal guardians of your children in the event that you and their father both perish.

A will certainly has its place in your must-have-documents file. When you die without a will, it is what is known as "intestate succession." This means your property is disbursed according to the intestate laws of your state. It's a cut-and-dried set of inheritance rules. I doubt you really want your assets to be handed out according to impersonal state laws.

This is all a will does for you. Now let me tell you what a will does not do for you.

▲ A will goes into effect only when you die. In the event that you are merely incapacitated, a will won't help you one bit.

▲ When you die with only a will, it does not make it easy to pass assets to your heirs. A will must be authenticated by a judge before it is considered to be valid. This happens via a court procedure called "probate." The probate process takes time and money.

▲ The wishes you lay out in a will can be overridden by other documents. For example, if you state in your will that your niece is to inherit your house, but you never bothered to remove your ex-husband from the title to the house as a joint tenant with right of survivorship, the house goes to your ex-husband. Your niece is out of luck.

So if a will is not enough, what do you need? You need a will and a revocable living trust.

Yes, you need both. I have read plenty of articles disputing this, but I will forever stand by my belief that you must have both of these documents. Back in the first chapter of this book, I identified the objective of building a healthy relationship with your money. To that end, you have to understand the reasons for making financial moves for yourself, so I will lay out my case and help you understand why I am passionate on this point. Then you can decide to agree with me, I hope, with confidence and certainty.

REVOCABLE LIVING TRUST

Of all the must-have documents, a revocable living trust is the most powerful, for, if set up correctly, it can take care of everything for you, both while you are alive and after your death.

If you have a revocable living trust, please pull it out now and make sure it includes everything I am going to discuss here. If you do not have a revocable living trust, keep reading.

Trust Basics

Let's begin with some definitions so we are all on the same page:

Revocable means that once you set up the trust, you can change it all you want. You remain in control. Nothing is set in cement.

Living means that it works for you while you are alive, unlike a will, which comes into effect only when you die. The terms and wishes expressed in your trust can also continue to apply after you have died.

Trust is simply the name of the document.

Settlor is the person who sets up the trust.

Trustee is the person or persons who have signing authority over every asset inside the trust. The trustee decides everything that happens to the money in the trust. If you are single, you can be the sole trustee. Or you and a spouse/partner can be joint trustees.

Successor Trustee is the person who takes over the management/control of the trust when the trustee dies or is no longer capable of making decisions. (We will cover this crucial issue, known as "incapacity," in a moment.)

Beneficiary is the person who is to benefit from the assets that are in the trust. Typically, while you are alive you remain the beneficiary.

Remainder Beneficiary is the person who "inherits" the assets in the trust when you die. (Put another way, whatever remains in the trust is what this person will get.) In your trust you can have multiple remainder beneficiaries; you may leave specific assets to specific people.

A Revocable Living Trust vs. a Will

Stay with me here—I just threw a bunch of new terms at you, but an example will show you how easy the trust makes things. Let's say my mom wants me to inherit the home she owns that is valued at $200,000. She has two choices: She can leave it to me in a will or leave it to me through a revocable living trust. Let's take a look at each scenario:

If my mom had only a will that stated I was to inherit the house: In almost every case, after a person dies, their will goes through a court procedure known as probate, which can cost as much as $2,000 in court fees simply to begin the process. But the costs do not stop there, as you will see below.

The process of probate first must establish that my mom's will is valid, so the judge will authenticate my mother's will and make sure that in fact she wanted to leave me her home. Once that is done, the next step is for the judge to help carry out my mother's wishes as expressed in her will—in this example, making sure that the deed to her home is transferred to my name. And since the deed to the home is only in my mom's name and she is no longer alive to sign it over to me, the judge will sign a court order transferring the house from her to me. That seemingly simple process can take months, if not years, and a lot of money.

The lawyer who handles your case is going to cost you, too. In some states, the legal fees to see a case through the probate process are set as a percentage of the estate; in other states, the lawyer is free to set his or her fee. The point is, your heirs will end up paying a lawyer to see your estate through the probate process. In the state of California, for example, the cost of shepherding a $200,000 home through probate would be $16,000. It's not uncommon for an heir to have to pay thousands of dollars to get their inheritance via a will. And what happens if you don't have the money to pay those fees? The lawyer who handled the case can file a lien against the house with the intention of forcing you to sell the home to raise the money to settle the bill.

See why I say the less money you have the more you need a revocable living trust?

If my mom created a revocable living trust and left the house to me upon her death: As the person who created the trust, my mother is the settlor. She also appoints herself the trustee—meaning she retains total control of everything in the trust. She places her home in the trust, and so the "owner" of the home is no longer Ann Orman. It is Ann Orman as trustee of the Ann Orman living trust. But remember, she is the trustee of the trust, so she has full control of all the assets held in the trust. She can sell the house, refinance the house, renovate the house—whatever she wants; she has the same control as before. And she still owes the same property taxes. There is no additional tax return that needs to be filed for the trust; your 1040 form is all that's needed. The house is held in trust for her benefit while she is alive, so that makes her the primary beneficiary. I, Suze, am her remainder beneficiary. Because her wishes were expressed in a trust and not a will, when my mom dies there will be no probate court, no judge, no waiting. Her house will pass to me with a minimum of work and expense. Along with the death certificate, I must sign an affidavit of the death of the trustee (my mom) and sign a deed that changes ownership from Ann Orman as trustee for the Ann Orman living trust to her successor trustee—me. This title change costs about $250, either through a title company or a lawyer. This whole process should not take more than a few weeks.

FUNDING THE TRUST

Once you create a trust, you need to take steps to change the title (ownership) of all the property to be held in the trust from your individual name (or, if you own it jointly, from both your names) to the name of the trust. This process is called **funding the trust**. If you do not fund your trust, all you have are words on paper— what's called an empty trust. An empty trust is completely useless. Therefore, you must change or have a lawyer change all the titles of your bank accounts, stock accounts, real estate, and all major assets into the title of the trust. Does this sound like a pain? Well, it's not fun, but remember, the idea here is to prevent major headaches later on. Once an asset's title is transferred to the trust, you are guaranteed that the asset will be managed and disbursed exactly as you have laid out in your document.

What Goes in the Trust

▲ Real estate
▲ Nonretirement investments

▲ Savings (bank and credit union accounts)

▲ Outstanding loans you have made that have yet to be repaid

What Does NOT Go in the Trust

▲ 401(k) and IRA accounts if you are married—it's better to make your spouse the beneficiary. (If you are single, you can make the trust the beneficiary.)

▲ Cars

WHY YOUR TRUST MUST INCLUDE AN INCAPACITY CLAUSE

If it is set up correctly, a trust is your answer to making sure your assets and financial affairs will be properly handled both upon your death and in the event that you become incapable of handling matters for yourself while you are still alive. To my mind, an incapacity clause is an absolutely critical feature of a trust. This section of your trust will grant your successor trustee—the person you designate—legal authority to handle your affairs should you become incapacitated. A good trust will also designate a backup trustee in case your successor trustee is incapable of fulfilling his or her responsibility as trustee. For example, let's say you and your husband have one trust and you are both each other's appointed successor trustee. That's fine. But sticking to our "hope for the best, but plan for the worst" credo, we need to deal with the possibility that you both could be severely injured in the same accident; so in that case, your successor trustee would take over.

A Trust with an Incapacity Clause vs. Durable Power of Attorney

Now, I'm sure that some of you have been told that if you have a durable power of attorney for your finances, you do not need a trust. It is absolutely true that another way to enlist someone else to handle your finances is to draft what is known as a durable power of attorney for finances and attach an incapacity clause to it. Just like a will, a DPOA looks so enticing because it can cost just a few hundred dollars for a lawyer to create, whereas a trust can cost $1,500 to $2,500 or more. What you think you are saving, however, could end up costing you way more. Even when a DPOA has an incapacity clause, many financial institutions (such as banks, brokerages, and mutual fund companies) don't like these documents one bit. Quite often, if you don't complete a DPOA issued by that institution, they will not honor it. And I don't think you want to go through the hassle of setting up different DPOA documents for every financial institution you do business with. I was happy to see that the November 2006 issue of *Kiplinger's* magazine featured an entire article on the shortcomings of a durable power of attorney. Finally, a magazine got it right! A far better option is a revocable living trust with an incapacity clause.

So now that you know why a will as well as a DPOA alone is not going to do the trick, you may be wondering why you have been told by lawyers that a will and a DPOA are all you need. Let me put it bluntly: *Any lawyer who says you need only a will and a DPOA, in my opinion, is not working in your best interest.* How is it in your best interest to go through the probate process? How is it in your best interest to possibly not have your DPOA honored?

Understand the economics at work here: A lawyer who recommends a will and a DPOA tells you that you're getting a great deal—he's only going to charge you a few hundred dollars to create those documents for you. You think, *What a doll—he's saving me so much money.* But what the lawyer doesn't make clear is that your heirs will likely need to spend thousands of dollars to hire a lawyer—*your* lawyer, he hopes!—to chaperone the will through probate court. What your lawyer is also not telling you is that if you have a DPOA, it could cost thousands of dollars in legal fees to get the financial institution to accept it. If you have a revocable living trust with an incapacity clause, there is no probate process when you die. No probate, no legal fees, and no problems getting a financial institution to let your successor trustee step in in case of an incapacity.

BUT THE TRUTH IS—YOU *ALSO* NEED A WILL

While the trust takes care of your big-ticket assets as well as a potential incapacity, you no doubt have plenty of smaller assets that have no title—your grandparents' china, a treasured pen, a favorite set of earrings. A will is where to spell out whom you wish to inherit these items. Your will also takes care of any assets that you didn't get around to transferring into the trust. Those assets will pour over to the will and be managed or disbursed exactly as you have laid out in the trust. That's why when you have a revocable living trust, your will becomes known as a pour-over, or backup, will.

Please note: Just because you have a pour-over will does not mean you should get lazy about formally transferring your major assets into a trust. In many states, if the value of the assets in your pour-over will are too large, they will not automatically pour over into your trust. Instead, your heirs will have to go through probate. At the risk of repeating myself: You want your major assets held in a trust.

Even if you don't yet have big assets such as a home of your own, I strongly recommend that you have a revocable trust as well as a will. Not only is a trust the best place to express your wishes should you become incapacitated, it is especially important for parents of dependent children. Single mothers need a trust so the appointed guardian will have the funds they need right away to care for the children. Also, the trust is crucial for the speedy disbursement of a life insurance payout to support the children if anything should happen to Mom. More on this just ahead.

FOCUS ON YOUR PURPOSE:
LOVE AND PROTECTION

Whether you work with a lawyer, or use a software program to create a will and a revocable living trust, the process of drawing up these critical documents cuts right to our emotional core: They force us to contemplate our mortality, and, when there are young children involved, they force us to decide whom we will want to care for them if, God forbid, we can't. I know this is gut-wrenching work, but providing for the well-being and care of your children is at the heart of your job as a parent. We may think that if something happens to us, our children will have their other parent to rely on, but that's not good enough protection. I need you to summon up the fortitude to contemplate the unthinkable: What if your children lose both their parents? Your will and trust must address whom you want to raise your dependent children and how you intend to provide for them in the tragic event both you and your spouse/partner die.

Choosing the right guardian obviously requires a great deal of thought and having potentially difficult and fraught conversations. What if you want to appoint your brother the guardian of your children, while your husband wants his sister to assume that role? There are no easy rules of thumb to follow, no one-size-fits-all advice I can dispense. It takes a lot of talking and soul-searching, and the conversations will be that much easier if you remain focused on one single purpose: what is best for the children. Step back and ask yourself: If both of us died, what environment would be best for our children? Who is best prepared to give them the emotional support they will need? (As we will cover in Month Five, your life insurance policy will take care of the financial needs of your children, so there is no need to choose a guardian based on how much money they have; this is an incredibly liberating factor that allows you truly to think strictly in terms of love and emotional guidance, rather than means.) Once you both arrive at a decision, you need to have a truly open conversation with that person(s) to see if they are in fact willing and able to assume this enormous responsibility. There is a big difference between acting out of obligation and acting out of desire.

Beyond the guardian issue, I find that the best way to think through what you need to include in your will and trust is to list every person you are close to in your life on a separate piece of paper and write down what you would want them to know, do, and have if you died today. Do you want to leave them money or a cherished piece of jewelry? Going through this process helps you organize both your thoughts and your assets.

Another decision you will need to make is whom to appoint the executor and successor trustee of the estate. This is the person who will be in charge of making sure that the wishes laid out in the will and trust are carried out once you die. This is another important decision; you want your executor and successor trustee to be someone you love and trust and someone you feel confident will be able to handle the job.

On my website is more information on the various tasks an executor needs to oversee. Please review these jobs with your executor and successor trustee to make sure he or she is ready to take on this responsibility.

I also strongly recommend that you make sure your family knows whom you've appointed executor so you can work through any ruffled feathers. While the executor doesn't make any decisions—he or she merely executes the decisions you have made—the executor does control the process. That can create some tension, especially when one child or sibling is chosen to be the executor over others; you owe it to those you didn't choose to explain your choice. Not defend it; just explain it.

WHAT YOU NEED TO KNOW ABOUT HOLDING TITLE TO YOUR ASSETS

Pay attention here: If all you have is a will, then how you hold title to your assets will override the wishes that you have in your will. Did you catch that? Here's an example to show you what I mean: Let's say you stipulate in your will that your daughter from your first marriage is to inherit your home. If, however, at the time of your death, your ex-husband is still listed on the title to the home as a joint tenant with right of survivorship, there are going to be problems. Upon your death, your home will immediately pass to him *even if your will states differently.* Your daughter can protest all she wants, but there is nothing—I repeat, nothing—she can do about it. If your ex wants to keep the house, he has every legal right to do so. Why is this? It's all about how you hold title. . . . Now I'll explain the various possibilities.

Joint Tenancy with Right of Survivorship (JTWROS)

This is one of the most common title traps women fall into: co-owning an asset as joint tenant with right of survivorship (JTWROS). This very popular form of ownership can lead to tremendous problems. One more time I'm going to say it: If you create a trust and properly fund that trust (transfer title to the trust), you completely sidestep this problem. But I know from experience that plenty of women go deaf when the topic of trusts comes up, and they insist they have everything set up just fine without a trust. Listen to me: JTWROS is not a great solution. You need a trust, plain and simple.

Anybody can own title to an asset in JTWROS—spouses, partners, mothers, and children. It is a very popular form of taking title to a home. When you hold title in JTWROS, you are a joint owner of the asset. When one of you dies, the survivor immediately inherits the other joint owner's share of the asset. No probate, no fees, nothing. That's what makes it look attractive. But as my own estate attorney, Janet Dobrovolny, describes it, JTWROS is like a winner-take-all contest where the survivor takes all. The person who dies first hands over complete ownership of that asset to the survivor. Now, I know that might sound fine if you and your spouse want to leave the property to each other, but be very careful here.

Second Marriages and the JTWROS Trap

Let's say you are in a second marriage. You and your husband both have children from your previous marriages. In your divorce you obtained outright possession of your home, and you intend to pass it to your children when you die. Your new husband moves into this home with you, and you decide to add him as a joint owner of the home, since he is going to pay part of the mortgage. So you have your lawyer change the title (deed) on the house from just your name to JTWROS, with both of you listed as the joint owners.

If you die before your second husband, you have possibly just disinherited your children. Remember, with JTWROS it is "survivor takes all"—if you die first, your share of the home passes to your second husband. It doesn't matter if you have a will that says your kids should inherit your home. The title to the asset—in this case, your home—trumps your will. Your second husband now owns 100 percent of the house and is under no obligation to leave it to your kids.

JTWROS with Your Kids

Have you read in a financial magazine that the best way to get around the probate trap is to add your children to the title of your home as JTWROS? Here's a horrible scenario to dissuade you from this option. Let's say you've added your daughter to the title of your house and she is in a car accident that is deemed to be her fault. The injured party sues her for damages. Her auto insurance doesn't cover all of the settlement. In that case, the courts can demand that any other assets she has be used to pay off the settlement. And guess what? The house—*your* house—is now one of her assets, so you could end up having to sell the house to settle her legal bill.

Do you see how a trust is a much better option?

A Note for Those of You Who Are Remarried

I realize that a major issue is how to make sure that when one of you dies, the surviving spouse can stay in the house and that eventually the home will be inherited by your children from a previous marriage. To do this, you want the home owned by your trust, but you also want to have a life estate recorded against the house. A life estate is a legal document that says the surviving spouse can live in the house until he/she dies or decides to move. At that point, the home will pass to the remainder beneficiary designated in the trust. In this scenario, your remainder beneficiaries would be the children from your previous marriage. So you have achieved both goals: No surviving spouse will ever be at risk of losing the house and your children will still inherit the home; they just have to wait a bit longer. I recommend hiring a lawyer to handle the life estate; for just $200 or so, a lawyer will create the document and make sure it is recorded with the proper government agency.

ADVANCE DIRECTIVE AND DURABLE POWER OF ATTORNEY FOR HEALTH CARE

It is beyond imagining for most of us to think there might come a time when we are physically incapable of speaking for ourselves. But if there is anything positive to have emerged from the

Terry Schiavo story that was in the news not long ago, it may be the fact that it illustrated this unthinkable situation in a vivid, terrifying, and tragic way. At the age of twenty-six, Terry Schiavo suffered massive cardiac arrest that left her in a permanent vegetative state. Her husband felt Terry would not want to remain on life support; her parents felt differently. Her husband and parents were locked in a lengthy and devastating court battle that polarized the country, lawmakers, and this poor woman's family.

It's one of the most unpleasant subjects I'm going to ask you to consider, but I hope I can convince you to face this subject head-on and create a single document that will express your wishes and give you the security of knowing you have protected yourself, unflinchingly, in one of the worst of the worst-case scenarios.

In the first part of this document, the advance directive, you clearly spell out the level of medical intervention you want in the event you become too ill to speak for yourself. A range of situations is addressed, including consenting to or refusing any care or treatment, such as pain relief; selecting health care providers and institutions; approving procedures; and directing end-of-life decisions, such as providing or withholding nutrition and resuscitation and organ donation. In essence, you are giving directions in advance, while you are able to make sound decisions, to your doctors or medical team. An advance directive is also known as a **living will**.

Now, the hard truth is that an advance directive/living will does not guarantee that doctors will automatically follow your wishes. In a survey published in the *Archives of Internal Medicine,* 65 percent of doctors reported they would not necessarily follow an advance directive if it contradicted what, in their view, was a preferable alternative approach. This is an excruciatingly difficult area for everyone to navigate—you, your loved ones, your doctors. In such situations, your durable power of attorney for health care becomes your voice.

In a DPOA for health care, you appoint someone you trust to become your agent in the event your illness prevents you from communicating your wishes. This person will literally speak for you, representing the wishes detailed in your advance directive in any discussions and debates with your doctors or family. You can appoint anyone to be your agent—a spouse, a friend, an adult child. I only ask that you think this choice through carefully. You want your agent to be not only someone you trust but a person who will be able to represent your wishes faithfully, even in the face of objections from family or medical advisors. You also want this person to want to do this job. I have been asked to be an agent by many people I am close to, but I declined; I knew I couldn't make the tough decisions that might need to be made one day.

Once you settle on your agent and that person has agreed to do it, I strongly urge you to discuss this with your entire family. Let them know that you have an advance directive, and whom you have appointed as your agent. This will help reduce the hurt and anger that often crop up when families are brought together in a tragedy and first learn of the existence of an advance directive and an agent. Discussing it ahead of time will also help your friends and family present a united front to your doctors.

WHERE TO GO TO GET IT DONE

A lawyer who specializes in estate planning can help you create the three must-have documents we've just discussed—a revocable living trust with an incapacity clause; a backup will; and an advance directive and durable power of attorney for health care. This same lawyer can also handle the job of funding your trust. There is no better way to find a good lawyer than to ask friends and colleagues for recommendations. Or, if you have used a lawyer in the past for other matters—say, a real estate lawyer who assisted you in a home purchase—ask him or her whom they recommend. You can also search for estate attorneys in your area on www.findlaw.com. (Use the search tool at the top of the page; enter "Estate" under "Legal Issue" and then your zip code.) Ask any lawyer you find through this method how long they have been practicing in the wills and trusts field. If they say anything less than ten years, find another attorney. Also, be sure to contact the state bar and find out if the lawyer you are considering has any record of being disciplined. If so, find another lawyer. I recommend you talk to at least three lawyers before settling on one. Here's what you want to hear:

▲ The lawyer specializes in wills and trusts.
▲ The lawyer wants to know all details of your financial life. A good lawyer will create personalized documents that address your exact financial situation.
▲ You will be charged a flat fee. No hourly billing.
▲ The fee includes the creation of all three documents.
▲ The fee includes funding your trust.
▲ The quote includes time to review the entire document—word by word—with you. Remember, power is knowing exactly what you have.

Here's an idea of what all this should cost: If you went to see my estate lawyer, Janet Dobrovolny, in Emeryville, California, and you were married, had two kids and one home, and the total value of your estate was under $1 million, she would charge about $2,500 to do all of the above.

I realize that is a lot of money, even though it is money well spent. So I want to let you know about another option. It was from the strong belief that everyone absolutely needs to have these documents in place that I developed my Will & Trust Kit—a software program that helps you create all three of these documents and is good in all fifty states. I relied on the expert advice of Janet Dobrovolny in creating it. In the kit she and I walk you through funding your trust yourself and provide you with every-thing you will need to change the title to your assets into the name of the trust. This kit contains all the must-have documents, including the advance directive and durable power of attorney for health care. I created this kit because I respect that everyone may not have $2,500 for a lawyer or may not feel comfortable working with a lawyer. The cost of the Will & Trust Kit is $13.50, and I would be more than happy if you shared it with your family and friends. It just takes one woman turning toward her money to change the lives of many.

REVIEW YOUR MUST-HAVE DOCUMENTS ANNUALLY!

Whether you create these must-have documents on your own or with the assistance of a lawyer, I am asking you to stay involved with these documents and review them once a year. You need to treat them with great care; they can protect you only if you make sure they stay current with your life.

Remember: When you acquire an asset, you will need to transfer ownership of it to the trust. It should be part of your thinking whenever you make a big-ticket purchase or open a savings or investment account. One exception here: It's not a good idea to put a car into a trust. Here's why: In the event you cause an accident, the fact that the title to the car is a trust might lead the other party to think you are wealthy—and may increase their desire to sue you for damages beyond what your insurance policy will cover. And speaking of insurance: If the trust owns the car, that can make it hard to get insurance (people are insurable, not trusts).

Make Sure Your Beneficiaries Are Up-to-Date

Every major asset you own should have a beneficiary—that is, the person or persons you want to have control of the asset when you die. When you transfer ownership of a new asset to your trust, you will also need to designate a beneficiary for that asset. In the face of life-changing events—marriage, divorce, births, and deaths—we may not always remember to update beneficiary information. So once a year I am asking you to review the following documents that contain designations for beneficiaries:

▲ life insurance policies
▲ regular investment accounts
▲ savings account/bank account
▲ 401(k) retirement account
▲ individual retirement account (IRA)

Make sure you are not creating inheritance problems by designating the wrong beneficiary:

▲ **Minor children are never to be your beneficiary.** Minor children are not allowed to take ownership of assets.
▲ **If you are married, do not make your trust the beneficiary of your 401(k) or IRA.** I know this may sound a bit confusing, given that I have told you how you must transfer your assets into a trust. But if you are married, your retirement accounts are one big exception. (If you are single, it is fine to make your trust the beneficiary.) The better move when you are married is to make your spouse the primary beneficiary of your 401(k) and IRA. You can then name your trust as the contingent (secondary) beneficiary of these accounts. It just makes life easier.

If you have an out-of-date or incorrect beneficiary, contact the company or institution that oversees that account—the life insurance company, mutual fund company, and so forth—and request the form to change your beneficiary.

When you complete the steps below and create these three must-have documents, you are seriously on your way to owning the power to control your destiny.

ACTION PLAN FOR MONTH FOUR

✔ Create a revocable living trust.

✔ Transfer all assets into the trust and appoint yourself as the trustee so you retain all control over the trust.

✔ Create a pour-over will.

✔ Choose a guardian for your children who is truly prepared and ready for the responsibility.

✔ Choose an executor for your estate who is ready and able to settle your affairs when you die.

✔ Create an advance directive that spells out your health care wishes.

✔ Create a durable power of attorney for health care that will allow your appointed agent to speak on your behalf with doctors and family if you become too ill to speak for yourself.

✔ Designate beneficiaries for all of your assets held in your will and trust.

✔ Review your will, trust, and beneficiaries once a year.

Month Five:
Protecting Your Family and Home

I WOULD BE THRILLED IF YOU . . .

. . . Chose the right type of life insurance for your needs.

. . . Had home insurance that truly protected you in the event your home was damaged or destroyed.

. . . Knew what isn't covered by a standard policy (flood, earthquake, hurricane, wind, for example) and what to do about it.

. . . Had a separate umbrella liability policy with at least $1 million in coverage.

. . . Purchased a renter's insurance policy if you are a renter.

. . . Purchased a condo insurance policy if you own a condo, co-op, or town house.

The first three months of the plan were about taking charge of the aspects of your financial life absolutely within your power to control—saving, improving your credit, investing, planning for the future. Month Four was about confronting some of life's more unpleasant what-if scenarios and making sure your voice and your wishes are clearly heard in the face of them. In this month, you're going to prepare for the "acts of nature" that are absolutely beyond your control by making some powerful moves to protect yourself, your home, and your family should they strike.

You tell me you would do anything to take care of your family and your home—and yet so many women struggle with the very notion of life insurance. It's right up there with trusts and living wills—I can't put a happy face on it and try to convince you that it's fun to confront your mortality. So I'm not going to waste time trying to make you warm up to the idea. Listen, life insurance is so very important, I am going straight for blunt: If anyone in your life is dependent on your income—be it children, parents, siblings, anyone—you must protect them with a life insurance policy. Not to do so is both careless and selfish. I don't care how uncomfortable it makes you to deal with the notion of dying; just think how uncomfortable your dependents will be if something were to happen to you or your partner tomorrow and they didn't have a life insurance policy to fall back on. Don't tell me you'd do anything to protect your family and then fail them on this most crucial point.

I am going to walk you through exactly what type of life insurance policy you need and how to calculate the amount of coverage that will protect your dependents. Don't worry about dealing with pushy insurance agents. All the information you need to put you in the power seat when purchasing a life insurance policy is right here. And some really good news: Life insurance is incredibly affordable. You are going to be amazed at how little it costs to buy yourself peace of mind.

Home insurance is the other major focus of this month. If you own a home, you no doubt have a home insurance policy. In my experience, however, the policy you have probably won't give you a big enough payout to cover a major loss. Over the past few years, insurance companies have slipped in a bunch of new rules and policy stipulations that can limit your coverage. Unless you read the super-fine print, you might not be aware of the changes. At the same time, far too many people who think they are protected in the event of losses from a natural disaster, such as Hurricane Katrina, find out after the damage is done that their policy does not provide the coverage they "assumed" they had. The bottom line is that simply having a home insurance policy isn't good enough. You must make sure that the specific level of coverage spelled out in your policy will indeed entitle you to the coverage you need. Assuming doesn't give you one ounce of protection. Knowing does.

I will indeed be thrilled if in this month you tackle your life insurance and home insurance. I am not going to ask you to add "auto insurance" to your To Do list for this month, but I do encourage you to go to my website and read up on what I think the correct levels of auto insurance coverage are, especially if you intend to buy a new car.

LIFE INSURANCE

Who Needs It

If there is anyone in your life (or your partner/spouse's life) who relies on your income, you need life insurance. That obviously includes any young children. It can also include your parents if you help them cover their bills or pay for some home-based care. It can even include a sibling or a friend for whom you provide financial support. The question you need to answer is: *If I were to die today (or if my spouse/partner were to die today), will those I/we support be able to take care of themselves?* If the answer is no, then you need life insurance.

Did repeating that question, even to yourself, make you squirm? I know it's a difficult truth to confront—that any one of us can leave this earth at any moment. Once again, I am asking you to spend some time on matters that are within your power to control once circumstances beyond your control take over your life. It is within our power to make sure that, should we die prematurely, the people in our life who are dependent on us will not have to struggle financially.

Special Note for Stay-at-Home Moms

One of the most dangerous mistakes families make is to insure only the breadwinner. As a matter of fact, it is just as important to have a life insurance policy that covers the stay-at-home mom, too. Think it through logically for a moment: If you were to die, your partner or spouse would probably need to hire someone to care for the kids. Where is that money going to come from? Even if your children are in their teens, help from a homework tutor or a driver to transport the kids to and from sports practices, music lessons, gymnastics, and so on, may be necessary. Remember, your partner or spouse can't be expected to work a full-time job and help one hundred percent of the time with the needs of the children. If something happens to you, the proceeds from the life insurance policy will allow your partner or spouse to hire caregivers without the worry of spending "extra money."

LIFE INSURANCE BASICS

How Long You Need Coverage

A life insurance agent will try to sell you on the idea that you need to buy a super-expensive policy that will cover you throughout your entire life. The reality is that very few of you ever need a "forever" life insurance policy—what the industry often refers to as a permanent policy. They are unnecessary and way too expensive.

Life insurance is meant to provide financial protection for those who are dependent on you at a point in your life when you have yet to build up other assets. Once you have accumulated assets that your dependents can fall back on—say, a sizable retirement fund or other significant investments—you no longer need life insurance.

Besides, people dependent on you today may not be dependent on you in ten or twenty years. A five-year-old child today is completely dependent on you. But twenty years from now, I expect—and so should you!—that your twenty-five-year-old child will no longer rely on you for financial support. (Please note: If in fact you have dependents with special needs and you anticipate that they will require your support forever, you may indeed want to consider a "permanent" type of life insurance. You should also talk to a lawyer who specializes in estate planning about setting up a special-needs trust.)

Therefore, for most of you, if the primary purpose of your life insurance is to protect young children you anticipate will grow into independent adults, then you probably do not need a policy that is longer than twenty to twenty-five years, max. Same goes with life insurance for a spouse or partner; chances are you only need to provide the protection until the assets you both have accumulated have grown large enough to support the surviving spouse if one of you should die prematurely.

How Much Life Insurance You Need

How rich a policy you need is another matter to figure out. But first, you'll need to have a few definitions under your belt.

Death Benefit: The money beneficiaries will receive upon the death of the insured. For example, a $500,000 life insurance policy has a $500,000 death benefit. In the event the insured person dies while the policy is active (what's called "in force" by insurance types), the beneficiaries of the policy will receive a $500,000 payout from the policy. A death-benefit payout is typically tax-free.

Principal: The actual amount of the death-benefit payout.

Income: The interest you can earn by investing the principal (the death benefit).

So how big a death benefit do you need? I recommend you buy enough so that your beneficiaries could live off the *income* alone and not have to eat into the principal.

Let's say you have a $500,000 death benefit. Your beneficiaries would have $500,000 to invest. If they invest it in a safe, tax–free bond that earns 5 percent annual interest, it would produce $25,000 a year in income ($500,000 × 5 percent). If that $25,000 is all they need to meet their living expenses, they could "live off the interest" without touching their principal. That means the next year, if they again earn 5 percent, they will get another $25,000 to cover their expenses.

But let's say they need $50,000 a year for their living expenses. If they earn only $25,000 in interest, they will need to dip into the principal and withdraw an additional $25,000 to cover their costs. So the following year, they will have only $475,000 in principal left ($500,000 − $25,000 = $475,000). If they earn 5 percent interest on that $475,000, it will generate just $23,750 in income; because the principal is smaller, so, too, is the interest it earns. If they need $50,000 to live on, they will now need to withdraw $26,250 of principal to add to the $23,750 in income in order to meet their target of $50,000. That will further reduce their principal ($475,000 − $26,250 = $448,750). You get the idea: If you don't have a big enough death benefit, your beneficiaries are going to have to dip into the principal to meet their living needs. And at some point, they are going to use up all the principal.

This is why I recommend buying a policy with a death benefit that is large enough so your dependents won't be forced to use the principal.

> **On my website I have a free worksheet that will help you carefully figure out the actual annual living expenses for your dependents.**

Aim for a Death Benefit That Is Twenty Times Your Beneficiaries' Income Needs

The wise way to do this is to add up the annual living costs for your dependents and then purchase a policy that is twenty times that sum. For example, if your dependents need $50,000 a year to cover their living expenses, I am asking you to buy a $1,000,000 life insurance policy. That is, a policy with a $1,000,000 death benefit. I know that sounds like a lot, but as I will show you in a moment, there is a special type of life insurance that is so inexpensive, even a $1,000,000 policy is quite affordable.

Now, most life insurance agents will tell you that your death benefit needs to be only five or six times your dependents' annual income needs. Their assumption is that your survivors will just need help for a few years, that eventually they will "get back on their feet." I certainly hope that's the case, but life insurance is not about hoping; it is about preparing for the worst. What if they are severely injured in an accident that takes your life? What if your survivors are so distraught they can't handle the pressure of a big-time career? Or perhaps it is your wish that if something were to happen to one of you, the surviving spouse/partner would have the financial flexibility to choose to not work.

It's for these what-ifs and others that I recommend purchasing a policy with a death benefit that is twenty times your beneficiaries' annual income needs.

Now, as I noted above, the goal is for your beneficiaries to invest the death benefit in a "safe" investment, and by safe I mean that there is very little risk of a huge drop in the value of the investment. As I write this in late 2006, you can earn about 5 percent on high-quality municipal bonds. (A municipal bond is also known as a tax-free or tax-exempt bond. All the interest you earn from the bond is free of federal tax and in many instances is also exempt from state and city tax.) I know that 5 percent might not seem like a lot, but what's important to understand is that a bond doesn't have the big downs (the risk that it will lose value) that stocks do. The trade-off for not having risk is that you don't have the chance for huge gains, either. That's a fine trade-off to make when your goal is to provide stable income for your survivors. The whole idea is that they can take the death benefit and invest it conservatively in bonds and earn enough income (the interest from the bond) to pay their bills. That's a lot better than if you leave them a death benefit that is so small they feel compelled to invest it more aggressively to generate the money they need. The problem with that approach is that there is no guarantee that aggressive investments in stocks or stock funds are going to consistently produce gains. So what will happen to your family if they invest the money in stocks and then the markets have a bad year or two?

Let me illustrate the municipal (tax-free) bond strategy with actual numbers. Let's say you determine that your family's annual income need is $50,000. Multiply that $50,000 by 20 and you have your target death benefit: $1,000,000. If your beneficiaries then invest the $1,000,000 in municipal bonds and earn a 5 per-cent interest rate, they will have an income of $50,000 a year ($1,000,000 × 5 percent (.05) = $50,000). That's exactly what you want them to have. And the best part is, they haven't touched their principal. The $50,000 annual payout is simply the interest that their $1,000,000 earned. They still have the $1,000,000 to keep invested. The longer they don't have to use the principal, the longer your death benefit will be able to help them live com-fortably without financial stress.

Of course, if money is tight and you have other financial goals that you need to address, you can scale back your death benefit from my ideal goal of providing twenty times your beneficiaries' annual income needs. But please aim to provide your beneficiaries with a policy that is at least ten times their annual income needs.

Life Insurance Available from Your Employer

Many employers offer life insurance as a part of their benefit plan. In some cases, the coverage is a benefit that comes at no cost to you, but more often this free coverage is limited to one or two times your salary. Any coverage beyond that comes out of your own wallet.

I don't recommend relying on employer-provided insurance. The amount of the free coverage is not nearly enough to meet my 20× rule, and buying more insurance through the company plan can typically cost you more than what you would pay with an individual policy. And the most important factor is that your "free" insurance is good only while you are an employee. When you leave your job—voluntarily or involuntarily—you lose the insurance coverage or have to pay a high premium to continue the coverage on your own. And what if your next employer doesn't offer a life insurance benefit? If you are older and have any health issues, it can become more difficult or more expensive to obtain coverage on your own. Relying on free life insurance available through work just puts you at risk of having to go out and get your own policy later in life, and that can mean paying a lot more than if you get your own policy today.

Buying life insurance through your employer may seem more convenient, but it's not necessarily a cost-effective solution. The premiums (annual costs) for group policies are typically higher than what healthy individuals can purchase on their own. And the premiums you pay on a group policy tend not to be locked in forever; your rate can increase as you age.

Bottom line: The safer and smarter move is to buy life insurance on your own today. If you are interested in the deal offered through work, at least compare your costs for that group plan to what you can qualify for in an individual policy.

STICK WITH TERM INSURANCE

Many life insurance agents make a living by confusing people into submission. They hit you with so many calculations and foreign terms, it makes your head spin. And then they pull out the big finale: the pitch that the life insurance policy they have for you is also a terrific way to build extra savings.

Fall for all of that and you will end up wasting thousands of dollars over the life of the policy.

Life Insurance Is NOT an Investment!

Here's the key lesson with life insurance: **You want a policy that is called "term life insurance."** Under no circumstance do you want "cash-value life insurance," no matter how fabulous the agent makes it sound. Cash-value life insurance is marketed as having the added allure of providing not just insurance, but also an investment/savings component. Cash-value policies go by a few different names: whole life, universal life, and variable life. I'm going to uphold my promise to keep things simple, so I will show great restraint and not tell you all the many reasons why I think these are an absolutely horrible choice for life insurance if your goal is simply protecting your dependents. (Just to be clear: That's all the vast majority of us ever need from life insurance.) Please do this one thing for me: Stick with term life insurance and nothing else.

Let's review:

Term life insurance: Yes!

Whole life insurance: No.

Universal life insurance: No.

Variable life insurance: No.

If you already own any type of cash-value policy, please go to my website for advice on whether it makes financial sense to get rid of that policy and replace it with a term life insurance policy. However, never cancel a life insurance policy until you have replaced it with a new policy.

Term Insurance Basics

Okay, so term it is. Now let's walk through the important components of a term life insurance policy:

▲ **The policy length can be tailored to your needs.** A term life insurance policy is true to its name: The policy lasts for a predetermined period of time (the term). This can be five years, ten years, twenty years, or even thirty years. If you die during the term, your beneficiaries receive the death benefit, typically tax-free. If you are still alive after the term expires, you no longer have life insurance, so when you die there is no payout to your survivors. That's okay, because you will choose a policy with a term that matches your needs; you only want the policy to be active during the term—that is, when you have dependents and have yet to build up sufficient assets on your own.

▲ **Low cost.** Term insurance is very affordable. It can be 80 percent cheaper than the cost of those cash-value policies I just forbade you from buying. With a term policy, the premium cost comes down to a few key factors: your age, your health, and the size of your death benefit. The younger you are and the healthier you are, the lower your annual premium.

▲ **Lock in a fixed premium.** I want you to buy a policy that is called "annual guaranteed renewable term." That means that as long as you continue to make your premium payments on time, your premium will not rise from year to year; it is a set rate. Nor can the insurance company cancel your policy.

▲ **Recently, a new type of term policy, called "return of premium (ROP) term" insurance, has become increasingly popular. I am not a huge fan, given the additional cost. On my website, I explain in detail why I think ROP term policies are unnecessary.**

Below are some examples of what a term life insurance policy for a woman might cost. These are just estimates, based on a nonsmoking woman in good health.

Twenty-Year Guaranteed Annual Renewable Term Policy: Estimated Premium Costs

Age of insured	$1,000,000 death benefit
35 years old	$60 per month
45 years old	$125 per month
55 years old	$333 per month

If you need just $500,000 of coverage, your monthly premiums will be roughly half the amounts shown above.

LIFE INSURANCE SHOPPING TIPS

If you have an insurance agent you enjoy working with or one recommended by a friend, then by all means work with that person—but first make sure the agent is in fact an "independent." That means the agent will shop around for the best policy for you among a variety of life insurance companies. An independent is better than a "captive" agent who sells only policies offered by one insurer.

One of the easiest ways to buy a policy is to work with an online firm. Two of my favorite term life insurance websites are SelectQuote (www.selectquote.com) and Accuquote (www.accuquote.com). The buying process involves answering a lot of questions about your age, health status, hobbies (for example, scuba diving and rock climbing can affect the price you will pay for coverage), your occupation, family health history, and so on. An agent will help you complete the paperwork. You may also be asked to take a new physical exam.

Buy a Policy from a Financially Solid Life Insurance Company

As part of the purchasing process, I insist that you ask your life insurance agent to show you the "safety ratings" for the insurance company. This is very important: You only want to take out a policy offered by an insurance company that will be in business ten, twenty, or thirty years down the line. To help consumers get a sense of a company's financial health, insurance companies have what is called a "financial strength rating," a grade that connotes how solid they are. The most widely known graders are the firms

A.M. Best, Moody's, and Standard & Poor's. You want to hear that your company's rating is at least A or better.

For more details on how insurance ratings work and the different grading systems given out by different rating companies, go to my website.

BENEFICIARY AND OWNERSHIP BASICS

When you purchase a life insurance policy, you will need to spell out who is eligible to receive your death benefit. You can have one beneficiary or multiple beneficiaries; you decide exactly who gets what.

Be aware, though, that this can be deceptively tricky. While it seems to make sense to name your spouse as a beneficiary, I have to ask: What happens in the event that you both die in an accident? Typically, the smoothest solution is to make your beneficiary your revocable living trust. That way the death benefit will automatically be paid out to the trust without its getting tangled up in the courts. And as we covered last month, you will have spelled out in the trust exactly how your assets are to be disbursed.

Attention Single Mothers: Beneficiary Alert!

If you are a single mother and this insurance is to protect your minor children, then you must make sure the beneficiary of this policy is not—I repeat *not*—your children or your estate. If you die and your minor children are listed on your life insurance policy as your beneficiaries, or even if you list your will or your estate as the beneficiary, there will be major problems ahead for them and their guardian. Let me explain why.

Life insurance companies will not make payouts to children under the age of eighteen (or their guardians). The insurance company will require the appointment of a guardian of the estate, even if you have named a guardian in your will. This is going to cost thousands of dollars. Once this is in place, most courts will then require the payout money to be invested in what is known as a "blocked account" in a bank. In a blocked account, the proceeds cannot be touched by anyone, including the guardian, without a court order. So every time your guardian needs money—let's say for your child's tuition—he or she will have to pay a lawyer to go to court and request the release of the money from the judge. In many courts, the judges don't make this a simple request to grant; they may require convincing that Social Security payments for the minors are not enough to meet the child's needs.

Now here's where it gets even crazier. Even though the courts are so strict about releasing money before your child is eighteen, once he or she turns eighteen, the money gets released all at once. Do you really want an eighteen-year-old to have complete control over a large sum of money? Need I say more?

All of this can be completely avoided—the legal fees, the probate judge, your eighteen-year-old in charge of a lot of money— if you follow the advice in last month's plan and create a revocable living trust. Once you have a trust in place, all you have to do is name the trust as the beneficiary of your life insurance policy. Then the life insurance company will automatically pay the death benefit out to the trust, where the money will then be managed exactly by the sucessor trustee according to the directions you have laid out in your trust. Yet another reason to have a revocable living trust.

ESTATE TAX ALERT!

If you are married, assets left to a surviving spouse are exempt from the federal estate tax. But when your estate passes on to someone other than a spouse, your heirs may owe federal estate tax. This is levied on estates valued at more than $2 million in 2007 and includes the value of investments, your home, and, yes, the death benefit on your life insurance policy. Add them all up, and if they exceed $2 million, your heirs may be stuck paying a stiff tax on part of their inheritance. If you anticipate that your estate will be above the estate-tax threshold, I recommend working with an estate attorney to set up what is known as an "irrevocable life insurance trust." The trust will be the "owner" of the policy. Your beneficiaries will still receive every penny of the death benefit, but the value of the policy is exempt from the estate tax. This kind of trust is very different from a revocable living trust. Make sure you do not confuse the two.

HOME INSURANCE

If you own a home, it is more than likely that you have home insurance coverage. Everyone with a mortgage has home insurance—your lender insists on it. But it's my experience that homeowners usually have no idea what level of coverage they have, and in fact the coverage they have is often full of coverage holes. Typically, you figure this out only once calamity strikes and you learn that your policy offers less coverage than you expected. By the time you say, "Oh, *those* holes . . . ," it's too late.

Given that your home is probably your single largest investment, to say nothing of its pull as the center of your family's life, I think it is worth a few hours of your time to make sure that you will be fully compensated if your home is damaged or destroyed. What very few people seem to grasp is that even if your home is destroyed, you are still on the hook for the mortgage. If your insurance policy doesn't come through and give you the coverage you assumed you had, then you could find yourself in a big financial fix. This is what so many Katrina victims had to deal with: insurance policies that didn't live up to their expectations.

I don't want that to happen to you.

To complete this task, you can either pull out a copy of your existing policy or get on the phone with your agent and have him or her confirm whether your policy includes the coverages I lay out below.

These are the key coverage components we will focus on:

▲ How much your policy will pay if your home is destroyed
▲ Whether your coverage automatically increases each year to keep up with rising home-construction costs
▲ What coverage you have in the event that you cannot live in your home if it is destroyed or damaged
▲ If you will be fully compensated for the loss of possessions
▲ If your policy includes personal protection in the event that you are sued

HOME INSURANCE BASICS

Know What's Not Covered

The most important part of your home insurance policy is what your insurer agrees to pay in the event that your home is damaged or destroyed in what is considered a "covered" loss.

That "covered" issue is where so many people get into trouble. Standard homeowner's insurance policies do not cover damage caused by a flood. Same for earthquakes. Your standard policy will also not cover you for hurricane damage. If you live in an area where any of those natural disasters are possible, then you must, and I mean must, get on the phone with your insurance agent ASAP and discuss what additional insurance is available for these "nonstandard" issues.

▲ **On my website is a detailed explanation of what types of insurance coverage are available for natural disasters.**

The other big problem homeowners run into is when the pay-out on a covered loss is less than they anticipated because they didn't understand the most crucial part of any policy: dwelling limit coverage.

Check Your Dwelling Limit Coverage

When you think about your home's value, it's natural to focus on what price it would fetch if you put it on the market today. But in terms of insuring your home, you need to focus on a completely different issue: what it would cost to rebuild it in the event it is seriously damaged or destroyed. The issue isn't what others might pay you for your home, it's what you are going to need to pay contractors and builders to construct/repair it. And given the cost of new construction and labor, that can end up being a lot more than you anticipate.

For example, a house that you could sell today for $300,000 (the market value) might take $200,000 to rebuild (the dwelling value) in the event that it is destroyed or damaged. The difference between the market value and the dwelling value is generally the cost of the land the home is sitting on. A plot of land in a nice neighborhood with a view of the ocean, mountains, or city lights will be worth quite a bit more than the same-size plot of land without these characteristics. It is important that you know what your land is worth and what a contractor will charge you to rebuild your home on this piece of land. Let's return to our example of a home with a $300,000 market value and a $200,000 dwelling value. If you find that your insurance policy covers you for just $150,000, you would be on the hook for the other $50,000 if you needed to rebuild completely.

You can find the amount of coverage you have on the first page or two of your policy. It is referred to as the dwelling limit coverage. Once you locate that dollar amount, I next want you to look in the same section for what type of dwelling limit coverage you have. The four possibilities are:

▲ Guaranteed replacement cost coverage
▲ Extended replacement cost coverage
▲ Replacement cost coverage
▲ Actual cash-value coverage

Make Sure Your Policy Is for Guaranteed Replacement Cost Coverage or Extended Replacement Cost Coverage

Guaranteed replacement cost coverage means your policy will pay whatever it costs to rebuild or repair your home to its condition before the loss, regardless of what the stated dwelling limit coverage is on your policy. That said, this high level of protection is not available in every state. Your next-best option—and the only option I want you to settle for—is extended replacement cost coverage. With this coverage, your maximum payout can be 120 percent to 150 percent of your stated dwelling limit coverage. So, for example, let's say you have insured your home for $300,000, but after it is destroyed in a fire, you learn that the rebuilding cost is going to be $360,000. If you have extended replacement cost coverage, you may be in luck: If the extended coverage is 120 percent of $300,000, your maximum payout is $360,000 (20 percent of $300,000 is $60,000; add that to the base $300,000 of coverage).

If your policy states that your dwelling limit coverage is just replacement cost, your maximum payout is limited to 100 percent of the stated value of your policy. In our example, that means the most you would be paid is $300,000. I don't think that's good enough. Please get on the phone with your insurance agent ASAP to discuss raising your coverage to extended replacement cost coverage.

And if your policy happens to state that you are insured only for actual cash value, you are definitely underinsured. Under no circumstance is this level of coverage okay. With actual cash value (ACV), your payout is based on the *depreciated value* of what needs to be repaired/rebuilt. Let's say your roof is fifteen years old and it is seriously damaged when a tree falls on it in a storm. If you have ACV, your insurer will base its payout on the value of a fifteen-year-old roof. Your payout will be only to restore the roof to the quality and condition of a fifteen-year-old roof. What good does that do you, when you need to pay a roofer to put on a new roof? You are going to end up paying the difference between the depreciated value your policy covers and what it takes to get the roof properly fixed. If your dwelling limit coverage is for ACV, you must—and I do mean must—call your agent and discuss increasing your coverage to at least extended replacement cost. Do it today.

Protect Your Possessions with Replacement Value Coverage

The same concept applies to how your policy covers you for damage to or loss of your possessions. The two basic types of available coverage are replacement value and actual cash value (ACV). Please check your policy to make sure that all your possessions are insured for replacement value. If your policy is for actual cash value, you are at serious risk of being underpaid when any possession is damaged or stolen. Need an example? Let's say you spent $4,000 on a plasma television two years ago and it is stolen. If you have ACV coverage, your insurer will pay you the value of a two-year-old plasma TV. For argument's sake, let's say that's just $2,000. That's probably not going to cover the cost of buying a new plasma TV. I don't want you to settle for insurance payouts based on the depreciated value of your possessions. Make sure you have replacement cost coverage so your payout will be based on what it costs you to buy a *new* replacement for a lost or damaged possession—because that's what you'll have to do.

Document Your Possessions

When it comes to getting paid for lost or damaged possessions, you can help make your case to the insurance company by documenting every item in your house. That means having a record of your possessions. If you have sales receipts, that's a great piece of evidence.

 On my website, you can use my free Home Inventory Tracker to create a complete record of the valuables in each room of your home, as well as upload photos of each item. Present this completely personalized inventory of your possessions to your insurance company and you will have a great bit of evidence that helps make your case.

Certain possessions, such as jewelry, art, and collectibles, may need to carry some extra insurance—what's called a rider or floater to your policy. On my website, I explain when you need to have this additional coverage.

Anticipate Rising Building Costs

You also want your home insurance policy to include an automatic inflation adjustment. With this feature, the dollar amount of your dwelling limit coverage will automatically increase each year to keep in line with rising construction costs. Typically, the annual increase is 4 percent or 5 percent.

Additional Living Expense Coverage

Let's talk about what happens if your home is destroyed, or is damaged so badly that you can't live in it. You're still going to owe mortgage payments on the home, so if you also need to move into another place until your home is rebuilt or repaired, you are facing a second set of housing costs. These costs can include such things as rent, parking, laundry, pet kennel costs, gasoline due to a longer commute, storage facility fees, and so on. That's where additional living expense coverage (also referred to as loss of use coverage) on your homeowner's policy can come to the rescue. It will help pay for living expenses that exceed your preloss living costs. But again, exactly how much and for how long will your insurer make these payments to you?

The ideal coverage is "no dollar limit and no time limit." If your policy offers only a limited payout (generally a dollar amount shown on your policy as a percentage of your dwelling limit) or stipulates that the payments will be made for just twelve months, I recommend talking to your insurance agent about changing your coverage. This will be especially important if you live in an area with a high cost of living. The cost to rent a home in your neighborhood, combined with all the extras you will need, could easily result in huge additional costs to run your household while you are waiting for your home to be repaired or rebuilt. Also, if you live in a city known to have a lengthy building permit approval process, being limited to just twelve months of payment from the date your home was damaged could result in your paying for several months of living expenses out of your own pocket.

Know Your Personal Liability Coverage

In the event that you are sued for accidentally hurting another person(s) or damaging their property, personal liability coverage will help pay for the associated legal costs and related damages. It can also cover the cost of any injuries caused by you, a family member, or even a pet, on or off your property. A standard homeowner's insurance policy will provide a maximum of $500,000 of personal liability coverage.

It's important to understand that someone who wins a judgment against you can "go after" your assets—that is, they can seek payment from the sale of your assets or can get a judge to authorize garnishing your wages (getting paid out of your paycheck). Having personal liability coverage can protect you from having your assets—or paycheck—raided. But pay attention to that standard coverage: The maximum on a standard homeowner's policy is just for $500,000. If your total assets—including your home—are worth more than $500,000, you need to discuss with your agent purchasing a separate personal umbrella liability policy. You can typically get a $1,000,000 policy for just a few hundred dollars a year.

ATTENTION RENTERS

You need home insurance, too. Don't make the mistake of thinking your landlord is on the hook for any losses or damages to your possessions. Your landlord is responsible only for damage to the physical structure, such as a leaky ceiling or faulty wiring. You and only you are responsible for damages to all the many things inside the walls. For example, if a major storm blows out the windows and the wind topples over your television, the landlord is responsible for fixing the window, not for buying you a new television.

A basic renter's insurance policy won't cost you more than $200 to $300 a year. Make sure that your possessions are insured for replacement cost, not actual cost value.

You also want to make sure that you have sufficient personal liability coverage—for the reasons stated above, but also because you could be on the hook for damage to your rental. For example, if you accidentally leave a candle burning and burn down your landlord's house or damage the apartment building, you are going to be asked to pay for the damages (and maybe even the injuries) your negligence caused.

If you have substantial assets that exceed the basic liability limit on your renter's policy, consider adding a personal umbrella liability policy.

ATTENTION CONDO, CO-OP, OR TOWN HOUSE OWNERS

Do not rely solely on your owners association's insurance! This "master policy" insures only the common areas, such as a clubhouse, swimming pool, stairways, and elevators. It does not cover the interior of your unit. Your counters, cabinets, appliances, the gorgeous bathroom tile you put in are not covered by the master policy. And, of course, you also want to insure all your personal possessions. You need your own individual policy to protect everything inside your unit.

You also want to make sure that you have sufficient personal liability coverage. If someone is injured due to your negligence or you accidentally cause damage to the condo, co-op, or town house building, you are going to be asked to pay for the damages. If you have substantial assets that exceed the basic liability limit on your condo policy, consider adding a personal umbrella liability policy.

HOME INSURANCE SHOPPING TIPS

If you need to purchase a new policy or are not satisfied with your current policy, first check with your auto insurance carrier to see if they offer home insurance or renter's insurance. Quite often, if you bundle both types of insurance with one company, you can get a premium reduction of 20 percent or so. But it also pays to do a bit of comparison shopping. It's smart to get premium quotes from at least three insurers to see who offers you the best deal. You can shop online at sites such as www.insure. com and www.2insure4less.com.

ACTION PLAN: SUMMARY FOR LIFE INSURANCE AND HOME INSURANCE

LIFE INSURANCE
✔ Get life insurance to protect anyone who is dependent on your income.
✔ Buy term insurance. Do not buy any other type of insurance.
✔ Opt for a guaranteed renewable term policy.
✔ For maximum protection, aim for a death benefit that is equal to twenty times the annual income your dependents need to cover their living costs.
✔ Make your revocable living trust the beneficiary of your life insurance policy.

HOME INSURANCE
Homeowners
✔ Make sure your dwelling limit coverage is updated to reflect the current cost of rebuilding your home if it were destroyed.
✔ Check that your dwelling limit coverage is either guaranteed replacement cost or extended replacement cost.
✔ Make sure your possessions are insured for replacement value; if you have just actual cash value coverage, you need to upgrade your policy.

✔ Confirm that your policy has an automatic inflation adjustment.

✔ Find out your coverage for additional living expenses. Ideally, you want a policy that will pay your living costs indefinitely while you rebuild/repair your home.

✔ Get a separate personal umbrella policy if your assets are valued at more than $500,000.

Renters

✔ Make sure you have your own personal renter's policy. If the value of your personal assets exceeds the liability coverage in your policy, buy an additional personal umbrella policy.

Condo/Co-op/Town House Owners

✔ Get your own personal condo owner's policy. If the value of your personal assets exceeds the liability coverage in your policy, buy an additional personal umbrella policy.

Beyond the Plan:
Knowledge = Power = Control

I want to congratulate you on all you've accomplished over the past five months. It was my intention to walk you through the actions that would bring you bedrock financial security. By that I mean that you would have a working knowledge of everyday financial tasks and terms as well as an appreciation for the ways in which planning for the unforeseen can alleviate feelings of anxiety and powerlessness. I hope you're feeling the effects of all you've done. You should feel proud, relieved, and, yes, empowered. As for me, well, I am pretty much thrilled.

So now you are facing life beyond the plan. I am well aware that some of you will be paying down your credit card debt for a good while, and others will need time to build up an emergency savings fund. Your retirement investing is going to have to be up front and center for all the years of your working life. In other words, I know that the work of The Save Yourself Plan is far from over, that it's a long-term commitment, but I hope you recognize that with every step you take you are building a healthy relationship with money. Remember the dysfunction we diagnosed back in the first chapter? As any good therapist will tell you, you can't heal relationships overnight; it takes hard work and determination and a vow to make it through the tough times. I hope it all hasn't felt like a grind to you; I hope you've begun to realize the benefits of living within these guidelines.

To be honest, though, I'm a little concerned about leaving you without an "Action Plan" for the months ahead. I don't want you to get overwhelmed or stuck, not knowing which financial goal you should grant priority over others. To that end, I have created an incredibly useful tool on my website.

▲ **The Action Planner on my website will ask you for some key information about your life and then suggest ordered financial tasks based on your specific situation (married, single, no credit card debt, lots of credit card debt, children, etc.).**

To give you a sense of what to expect, here is a basic order of priorities that proceeds from the assumption that you have funded your 401(k) enough to qualify for the maximum employer match:

1. **Pay off high-rate credit card debt.** Any extra money in your paycheck first goes to paying off your credit card bills.

2. **Boost your emergency cash savings *and* max out on your Roth IRA (or traditional IRA you intend to convert).** If you are still working toward building an eight-month cash stash, plow more money into the account. If you are currently investing less than the annual limit in your IRA, increase your contribution. In 2007, you can invest up to $4,000 in an IRA if you are under fifty years old. (If you are over fifty, you can invest $5,000.) If you want to supercharge both your emergency savings and your IRA, do the 50-50 split: Whatever extra money you have to invest each month should be divided between the savings account and the Roth.

3. **Save up for a home.** If you are renting and it is your goal to own a home, create a new separate savings account just for your down payment, and send extra money into the account each month.

 Wondering how to figure out how much house you can afford? Go to my website for help making the proper calculations.

4. **Increase your 401(k) contributions.** If you have no credit card debt, your emergency fund is in place, you are under forty-five years old, and you are maxing out on your IRA, you should use any extra money to add more to your 401(k). Investing enough to qualify for the maximum employer match is bare-minimum investing. Ideally, you want to invest as much as you can manage. If you are under fifty, you can invest up to $15,500 in 2007; over 50 and you are allowed to stash $20,500 in your retirement account.

5. **Put money into a college fund.** Please take a look at items 1 through 4 on this list. Everything that came before the kids' college fund was about achieving financial security for yourself. The emergency cash fund. The retirement savings. The home you truly own. Taking care of all of that is just as much about your children's well-being as it is about yours. The reality is that when your children become adults the financial demands on their life are going to be heavy enough without their also having to worry about taking care of you.

 If you are ready to start a college fund, you can get advice on the right investments—including a discussion of 529 plans and Coverdell savings accounts—on my website.

It's my hope that in the months and years ahead you'll capitalize on the momentum you've built up and want to do more: to move from being a saver to an investor; from a renter to an owner; from being financially insecure to financially powerful. I hope that you'll not only maintain your financial literacy, but increase it. Because this is what I firmly believe: Knowledge = Power = Control. With that in mind, here then is my **I WOULD BE THRILLED** list for life beyond the plan.

I WOULD BE THRILLED IF YOU . . .

. . . Read one financial magazine a month—be it *Money*, *Kiplinger's*, or *Smart Money*. Any one of these three would be fine.

. . . Picked up the *Wall Street Journal* once a month and looked it over. No need to read the financial tables; just look through the articles and see if anything catches your eye.

. . . Watched CNBC at least once a month to see what you can learn.

. . . Tuned in to Bob Brinker's *Moneytalk* nationally syndicated weekend radio show. He's also on XM and Sirius satellite radio. I think he's fabulous. You can find your local station and airtimes on his website, www.bobbrinker.com.

. . . Subscribed to Bob Brinker's *Marketimer* newsletter and bought some of the mutual funds he suggests.

. . . Talked to your daughters and granddaughters about money and made a financial family pact to learn as much as possible together.

. . . Created an investment club where you could talk freely and educate yourself about money.

. . . Loved dealing with your money as much as you love watching *Dancing with the Stars*.

Okay, so it's a wish list. I know that reviewing your beneficiaries annually can't compete with *Dancing with the Stars* in entertainment value, but you can't blame a girl for hoping. . . .

MAKE A PROMISE TO YOURSELF

I have a saying: The easiest thing to do in life is to forget, and the hardest thing to do is to remember. Now that you've worked your way through the five months of The Save Yourself Plan, please make a promise to yourself: You will never forget how good it felt each month as you started to take control of your destiny. And remember how incredible it felt at the end of each month to know you'd completed all the crucial steps to building security. I know that if you keep that sense of accomplishment and confidence close by, it will be all the motivation you need to stay on this path—moving forward!—for the rest of your life. You are too powerful to ever go back.

7

THE COMMITMENTS

The primary goal of this book is to heal the relationship you have with money, which has been our focus until now. But you don't exist in this world alone with your money. You are at the center of a web of relationships, and navigating them can be very complicated, especially when money is involved.

The vast majority of women who call in to my television show have problems not with money per se, but with relationships. The money problem is usually a symptom or a consequence of the relationship problem. In previous chapters, we talked about how women equate giving with a show of love, so when we love a person or a cause so much, our nurturing soul directs us to give, give, give. We give money, even if it means digging into home equity lines of credit, ringing up more debt on credit cards, or cosigning loans. We say yes to whatever is asked of us, rather than stopping to assess the impact it will have on our lives emotionally and financially. We tend to let other people set the agenda for us. They tell us what they need, and we put their needs front and center, even if it means sweeping everything we need aside. We are more committed to helping others than we are to helping ourselves.

Are you one of these women?

- ▲ The woman who knows deep down that an emergency savings account is the core of financial security, but when her sister falls behind on the mortgage, car, and credit card payment for the umpteenth time, she once again cleans out her only savings account because she can't imagine not helping.
- ▲ The wife who knows deep down that the equity she and her husband have in their home is an asset that should be saved and protected, not spent, but when her husband has his midlife crisis and announces that he wants to quit his job to pursue a start-up business, she doesn't have the heart—or courage—to say no.
- ▲ The woman who knows deep down that her best friend is a financial train wreck but still agrees to cosign a car loan for her, which means most likely she will end up paying for that car even though she cannot afford to do so.
- ▲ The daughter who sends $500 a month to her parents to help them with their bills, even though that means she doesn't have the money to cover her own expenses.
- ▲ The stay-at-home mom whose weekly money is being used to pay the bills with increasing frequency and yet she says nothing, though she has no money of her own.
- ▲ The bride-to-be who is too afraid to ask for a prenuptial agreement or talk about money before her wedding date, for she thinks it will take the romance out of the relationship.
- ▲ The beloved employee who kicks in $25 every time she is asked to contribute to a coworker's wedding present, birthday party, or Christmas celebration, even though it puts her behind in paying her own bills.

▲ The mother who continues to bail out her adult children from their mistakes.

What I find both moving and encouraging is that women who find themselves in these kinds of situations realize, on some level, that they are just as much the problem as those who are making the money demands on their life. Loving someone you are committed to does not mean that you always have to give money; it simply means you have to be able to give of yourself. And giving of yourself takes us right back to the eight qualities of a wealthy woman, for it takes more power to say no out of love than to say yes out of weakness. I want you to consider this concept for another moment, because it's a big one, ladies. **It takes more power to say no out of love than to say yes out of weakness.** This notion is at the very heart of establishing a healthy relationship with your money.

BE AS COMMITTED TO YOURSELF AS YOU ARE TO OTHERS

As straightforward and logical as it may seem to talk to those you love from a place of power and honesty, in reality it is probably one of the hardest things you will ever have to do. Saying no to someone you love is difficult. It is easier to make a mess of our finances by saying yes all the time than to live with the fear of what the word no will do to our relationships. But as every woman who has fallen into this habit will tell you in hindsight, making money decisions in the hope of saving a relationship always backfires. That is why we go right back to the mainstay of keeping *you* in a healthy relationship with your money. Are you doing what is easy or are you doing what is right?

AN EXERCISE

Right here and right now I'm asking you to make this commitment to your relationship and to yourself. This is what I want you to do. Get out a piece of paper and a pen and write down the following words:

From this moment on, when it comes to my money and my relationships, I promise always to do what is right rather than what is easy.

Sign it and date it. Tape it where you will always see it—whether that's on your mirror, computer, or dashboard (or all of them)—or stash it in your wallet. Before making any moves with money—your own money or money that you share with someone—I want you to ask yourself, "Am I doing this because it's the right thing to do or because it's easy?"

It's easy to tell your boyfriend you'll lend him money that you don't have. It's easy to let your parents continue to get into financial trouble. It's easy to avoid the topic of a will or trust with your husband because he's afraid of his own mortality. It's easy to take your kids to the mall and buy them another $150 pair of jeans. But doing what is easy is not how you build a healthy relationship—with people or with money.

WHERE YOU ARE IN YOUR RELATIONSHIP

You and Your New Honey

I want to start with the dating scenario: You meet a great person, things are heading into "serious" territory, and you are thinking of moving in together. No matter if you are twenty-two and about to share a studio apartment, or forty-two and about to share the beautiful home that you own outright, you must talk money before anyone moves anywhere. How will you split the rent? Or the mortgage payment, or the grocery bill? What if he or she makes three times what you do?

Those are all important questions . . . yet having the money talk is always the last thing women want to do. And that invariably causes relationship problems down the line. Talk now and I guarantee you will build a stronger relationship.

I know your biggest concern is how you will split the closet space, but what should really be at the top of your list is how you will split the bills. Too often I hear of couples who move in together and then discover they had completely different assumptions about how they would share the finances. Assuming is not the way to go. Before anyone makes a move, make sure you agree on how the bills will be split.

And do not automatically assume that 50-50 is the right answer. What if you make $100,000 and your partner makes $50,000? Is it fair to split everything 50-50? Here is what you are to do:

▲ Add your monthly take-home pay to your partner's monthly take-home pay. That is your total household income. Now divide your total monthly expenses by your take-home pay and from that you will derive a percentage. That percent is what each of you should contribute to your monthly joint expenses.

  Here's an example. Let's say your after-tax pay is $7,000 a month and your love brings home $3,000 a month. Your total household after-tax income is $10,000. Now add up all the expenses you have each month that keep the household running. Let's say those expenses for utilities, rent, phone, and so on, come to $3,000 a month. Divide $3,000, your joint expenses, by $10,000, your joint take-home income, and that will give you 30 percent. That means that you each have to put up 30 percent of your take-home pay toward expenses, or

$2,100 from you and $900 from your love—equal percentages, not equal amounts.

▲ Set up a joint checking account to pay for household bills. Yes, keep your own checking account, but set up one together. This is a great testing ground for your money habits. You know from the first month of The Save Yourself Plan that I want you to sit and pay the bills together. That means that one week before your appointed bill-paying, both of you are to have deposited your share of the monthly expenses into that account. There are to be no slipups and no excuses. As far as I am concerned, this is a litmus test to see how financially responsible your love interest is, and for your love interest to gauge the same about you.

Share Your FICO Scores

I have to tell you, this is the quickest and most revealing window into the financial makeup of your life-partner-to-be. I know this isn't going to win me any romance awards, but I firmly believe that any person who is financially irresponsible is more likely to be emotionally irresponsible in a relationship. For that matter, if you are the one with a messy credit history, you owe it to your potential life partner to come clean. Now, if you or your life partner has a low FICO score, the relationship isn't doomed. I am in no way saying a FICO score below 760 is the new relationship litmus test. The point is that you must both be honest and open about your financial situation. Ultimately you should support each other in terms of stepping forward and fixing whatever financial mistakes you have made in the past. Lasting love and commitment is dependent on how we get through the messy stuff in life. But when the mess is so deep and ingrained, you also need to have the courage to exit a relationship—not only because it will financially drain you, but because it is so emotionally costly.

A caller to my television show provides a living, vivid example. Lynn is in her forties and is caring for her elderly father. She has managed to take care of herself and her father without falling deep into debt. She is financially responsible, but at the same time she has a boyfriend who is a financial wreck. He has $30,000 in credit card debt, no money saved, and is pressuring Lynn into letting him move in with them. Lynn turned to me because she didn't know what to do. She kept telling me she loved her boyfriend, but she knew that his financial irresponsibility was a huge problem. I asked Lynn what I ask so many women in situations like this: "You tell me you love him, but do you really like him?" Normally, there is a sigh or a moment of silence. And then they tell me no. No, they don't like him, because he refuses to be financially responsible and reliable. And they resent all the pressure that puts on them and on the relationship. That is not a commitment worth keeping. Plain and simple. It took Lynn a few years, but she eventually broke up with her boyfriend. If you ask me, she did what was right—and it wasn't easy.

The Marriage/Commitment Conversation

Given that women on average are marrying/partnering for the first time later in life, chances are that when you do find the right person, you may already have a lot of financial baggage in the form of assets and debts. And so, too, may your fiancé or life partner. The basic rule is that you are jointly entitled to assets accrued during a marriage and you are on the hook for debts accrued during the marriage. Anything you bring into the marriage is not automatically shared. Yet I have seen so many women run into trouble by switching titles or not clearly spelling out what is theirs—and not ours.

I've taken a strong position on this for a long time: I believe in prenuptial agreements. If marriage is not an option, then in those cases I believe in cohabitation agreements. These documents have never been more important than they are now, given the career success so many women bring into their relationships. If you are remarrying, this becomes even more important. I am not suggesting that either of you hoard what is yours, but with so much on the line, I want you to state clearly to each other what you expect to remain separately owned and what you expect to become shared assets or property.

 On my website are suggestions of what should be covered by a prenuptial agreement or a cohabitation agreement. You'll even find forms there that you can download and use as a template for your agreement.

You and Your Spouse/Partner

It's so easy to hand over responsibility for financial matters to your partner. History works in favor of that, as handling the money was always viewed as the man's domain. But it's the twenty-first century, my dear ladies. It's time to let go of that convenient excuse. I see far too many women lazily fall into these stereotypical roles because the money stuff mystifies them or doesn't interest them. Being in control of your financial destiny requires that you be an active participant—not just by paying bills, but in overseeing your investments, too. Take this step and I think you will be surprised how this helps your relationship.

I have a funny story to tell you. When I decided to write this book, I began my research and sought out many experts and professionals who specialized in working with women. After speaking to many of them, I decided it was time I stopped asking questions in general about women and started asking personal questions about how these women handled their money themselves. The answers I got startled me, to say the least. One brilliant academic admitted that her life partner handled their finances—she just didn't want to deal with it; she tried to read the statements, but none of it made any sense to her. Besides, she trusted him to take care of everything.

"So let me get this straight," I said. "I have just been on the phone with you for over an hour and you can tell me every hormonal, biochemical, and psychological reason why women behave in certain ways, yet you don't feel you have what it takes to understand money?" Well, you can imagine that she got a (compassionate) earful from me. To repay the favor of the time she spent on the phone with me, I offered to review all her financial statements to make sure that her partner knew what he was doing with their money.

The next morning, my fax machine started spitting out one statement after another, along with a note that explained that after our conversation, the professor couldn't stop thinking about what I had said to her about being in control of her own money. So that night, at her request, her partner walked her through every financial statement and explained everything to her. He was thrilled, finally, to have her involvement, and she was so happy, too, because for the first time she really understood what was going on in her financial life. Her partner had, in fact, done a great job with her money, so I called to tell her that. When she picked up the phone, she told me that ever since that night she felt like she had a healthier relationship—with her money and her man. He actually loved and respected her more for taking this step. She also confessed that their sex had never been better—if only she'd known, she'd have gotten involved with her money sooner. (See what I mean about people telling me everything?)

If your partner has been nudging you for years to show interest in your financial life, then it will be easy for you to put this book down and tell him you are ready to become his financial partner, too. He will no doubt be excited to have you on board at last. A good place to start this new phase of your relationship is with The Save Yourself Plan; you can use that as a template to learn about what your husband or partner has already done for the family.

Please approach this as a collaborative endeavor. You are not putting him to the test or questioning his choices. He is your partner, your lover, your life mate. Respect that bond. And if you do find that some decisions he made run counter to the advice in The Save Yourself Plan, then talk it through. No accusations. He deserves the "no shame, no blame" treatment as much as you do. I hope your guy is a financial whiz and made all the right moves for your family, but quite often I see women mistake the enthusiasm men have for handling finances for expertise. So if your man made a few mistakes, no worries. The point is that you are now a team that can make the necessary financial adjustments.

Trouble Ahead

Now, if you are years into a relationship with someone who actually likes the old-fashioned dynamic of being in total control of the money, you obviously want to be sensitive to that. Take the time to explain to him that your becoming involved with the finances is not about him giving up power or questioning his abilities. It is about your need to be knowledgeable and involved. To *share* the responsibility with him.

If your husband resists, however, I think you need to wonder what is really going on. It is important that you have a totally open relationship about every penny you have and you do not have. I am asking you to settle for nothing less.

 I hope you never need to access this information, but on my website, I have a virtual mini seminar on the key points you will need to be aware of and the actions you must take

to protect yourself if your marriage should end in divorce. If you find yourself in a troubled relationship, I would encourage you to visit my website and start reading up *now*. Be prepared—arm yourself with knowledge before events overtake you.

Home Finances and the Stay-at-Home Mom

This is one commitment that women get wrong time and time again: stay-at-home moms who equate a paycheck with power. Talk about putting yourself on sale . . . Do you know how often stay-at-home mothers tell me they don't know how to ask their husbands for money to buy something the family needs or—God forbid—something for themselves? Curiously, they tend to be responsible for the monthly bill paying but not the family's long-term investment strategy. The thankless job is theirs, and when there isn't enough money to cover the monthly expenses, they are the ones made to feel guilty. Often the problem is that there simply isn't enough money coming in to cover all the bills, not that the stay-at-home mom wasn't financially responsible.

But women put up with this dynamic. It's my guess that they have an underlying sense of guilt or gratitude that the husband is the one working while they get to remain at home. I want every stay-at-home mother today—and those of you who think you may go this route someday—to listen up and listen good: The job of the stay-at-home mother is equal to the job of the breadwinner. Please read that again. Your job is as important, as vital, and as necessary as that of your husband who earns a paycheck.

When you both value the incredible work it takes to run a household, it completely changes how the finances work. No stay-at-home mom should ever have to ask for money or feel guilty about spending money. To behave that way presumes that the money coming in is "his." It is not his, it is yours. Both of yours.

When you see that paycheck as being jointly yours, you suddenly don't need to ask for anything, right?

Now, that said, you both must make the commitment to figuring out how your family will be able to handle life on one paycheck. You may well want to be a stay-at-home mom, but that doesn't automatically translate into its working out financially. Both you and your husband/partner need to work together to see what makes sense for your family. If you cannot survive on one income, that is not your husband's fault. This is a two-way street; you both share responsibility for figuring out if this is financially feasible. Maybe you need to work part-time. Or maybe you need to consider living in a less-expensive area. The point is that as a team you both must take responsibility for whether you can live comfortably on one income.

If you both agree that it is financially feasible for one parent to stay home, you need a strategy so you are never asking your husband for cash. My recommendation is that you both agree that whatever money is left over at the end of each month—after paying the bills, funding your retirement savings, and so on—is to be evenly split. In other words, the "extra" money goes into your separate checking accounts. And you are both free to spend that money as you wish. If you have yet to build up your own private savings fund, that is where you find the money to get it going. But remember: If your husband wants to use his share of the extra money to buy some electronic toy, or a ski trip with the guys, he is free to do it. The point is, if you have collectively made sure all your family's financial obligations are met, then beyond that point you should both be free to spend (or save) your share of the extra money however you want.

Now, what happens if there is no extra money whatsoever? Then both of you need to make equal sacrifices. Just because your husband leaves the house to go to work doesn't mean he has extra privileges to spend money. If you don't have the money to go out for lunch with your friends, he can't go out to lunch with his coworkers. You've got to share the burden equally. Remember, the one who brings home the paycheck doesn't have the power to decide how it's spent. The two of you who share that money have equal decision-making power. Give the relationship power over the money—do not make money more powerful than the relationship.

Woman as Breadwinner

The statistics show that increasingly women are outearning their husbands—a phenomenon unthinkable in our mothers' generation and so newsworthy even now that it was a trend story on the cover of several national magazines. Yes, the woman as breadwinner is another example of how history is being rewritten in our lifetime. This radical shift in our society means that while the rules are changing for women, they are also necessarily changing for men, which creates new problems for men and women alike.

Whether their paycheck covers the household expenses or not, men today still carry the emotional and financial burden of the traditional role of breadwinner. When both spouses work but the wife outearns her husband, I can assure you that no matter what is said, earning less than his wife affects a man's sense of his own masculinity. He may say it doesn't matter, he may say he's fine with it, but trust me—it is hard for a man when his friends make more than he does, when his friends have fancier cars or bigger houses, so imagine how hard it is for him to be truly at peace with the notion that his wife brings home a paycheck bigger than his. It takes a mighty big and enlightened man to be comfortable with this role reversal.

Now, what I've seen happen time and again in these relationships is that the wife tends to disown her power and downplay her role as breadwinner. She doesn't talk about it, she backs away from any acknowledgment of it, because she doesn't want her husband to feel bad or to feel "less than." In fact, this kind of behavior enables the man in creating a dysfunctional relationship of his own with money! Many times I've seen men in this situation get themselves in trouble financially. Spending money becomes a matter of pride, and so by whatever means necessary—borrowing against credit cards, taking out a home equity line of credit, whatever it takes—having money to burn like a big shot becomes all-important. (Interestingly, stay-at-home dads don't seem to suffer from this problem. Once a man makes the decision to run the household, that becomes his job; it is *his choice* to raise kids rather than funds—and therefore it's easier to reconcile to himself and others.)

The solution to this problem? Start talking. Understand that no matter what he says, his thoughts are not in harmony with his words and actions. It is your job, ladies, to help your man rewrite history for himself. Let him know he's not the only one who feels uncomfortable; let him know that you're in this together, that you're both blazing a new trail here. Most important, it is critical that you both understand that this change won't happen overnight. So keep talking; take this matter out of the darkness and into the light. Keep talking until his and your thoughts, feelings, words, and actions are in perfect harmony.

You and Your Kids

Do you know how many adult children come to me with a mix of anger and sadness about how they feel their parents let them down financially by not being honest? Children who suddenly learn in their twenties and thirties that Mom and Dad don't have any retirement savings because they plowed every penny into their children's college education. Or even worse, they financed college with a home equity line of credit they intended to pay

off once the kids were out of school, but then they were suddenly pushed into early retirement and couldn't find a new job
at fifty-five. So now the children are worried that Mom and Dad
will lose the house if they can't repay the loan, and then where
will they live?

I also hear from college kids who find themselves with $3,000
in credit card debt. At freshman orientation, they were practically
assaulted with offers to open up a credit card account, but no
one ever took the time to teach them how to handle that card
responsibly. As angry as I am at credit card issuers for preying on
clueless college kids, I lay a lot of the responsibility on the parents:
Before you send your kids out into the world, you need to teach
them how to be financially responsible. Here's what it takes:

▲ **Be honest**—with yourself and with your kids. Being a good
   parent is not dependent on what you spend on your children.
   If you do not have the money for the $150 pair of jeans or the
   latest video game, you must tell them that. Simply putting it
   on your credit card is dishonest: It prevents you from moving
   toward a life where you are financially secure, and it gives your
   kids the false impression that they can have whatever they
   want. That child ends up being miserably in debt as an adult,
   because he or she knows no better.

   Be honest, too, about paying for your children's college education. As far as I am concerned, there is no more loving gesture you can make for your children than to make sure you will
   have financial security in retirement. That is your priority. If
   you simply don't have the money to save for both retirement
   and their college costs, then retirement must be your focus.

   Do not feel guilty about this and do not hide it. You must
   discuss your intentions with your children as early as middle
   school—not to scare them or depress them, but to motivate
   them to do well so they have the best chance of qualifying for

grants, aid, and scholarships. Maybe they will have to get a part-time job so they can create their own college fund. Let them know they—and you—will need to take advantage of college loans. This should truly be a family affair. There is no blame or shame in not being able to write a blank check. Your honesty about the situation, and your ability to respect your children by involving them early, is to me the essence of being a good parent.

▲ **Be a teacher.** Our ability to handle money responsibly is not something we are born with. It is something we learn. And unfortunately, our educational system does a lousy job of teaching personal finance to kids; the reality is that it is rarely part of any school curriculum. So the job falls entirely to parents. You must teach and show your kids the value of money.

Once a child turns twelve or so, I think it is wise to involve your kids in the family finances. Have them sit with you as you pay the bills—not to make them feel grateful for what you provide, but so they have an understanding of what life costs. Here's an idea: Let your child guess how much the monthly electric bill is. You might find that he or she will think twice before leaving lights or the TV on after leaving the room.

One of the most important lessons you can impart is how to handle credit cards. If you have a strong FICO score, I recommend adding your child to an existing account as an "authorized user" once he or she reaches the age of fifteen. That entitles your child to use the credit card while you get the bill; so you have the opportunity to educate, set limits, and so on. It also entitles your child to start building a credit history based on your FICO score. That can be a huge leg up for your kids once they graduate from college. With a solid FICO credit score, they will have an easier time renting an apartment, and chances are they won't have to make big deposits to open accounts with the gas company, the cable company, the cell phone company, and so forth. A strong FICO score might even tip the scales in their favor when they are applying for a job; employers often check the FICO scores of job applicants to assess their general reliability.

If you do not have a strong FICO credit score, I want you to get your child a secured credit card that is in their name only, and make sure the deposit is set low—at $250 or so. Just like a driver's permit, this card is their testing ground where they learn how to spend responsibly—ideally, with money they earn either from a part-time job or doing extra chores around the house. (And I do mean extra. I don't think any child's allowance should be based on performing basic chores. It is important that you teach your kids that certain responsibilities are expected of them period—without the incentive of an allowance. That's their contribution to the family. Beyond those jobs, you can then create an allowance that covers additional tasks. For example, perhaps setting and clearing the dinner table is a standard job they perform as a member of the family, but washing dishes twice a week is something that helps them earn their allowance.)

You and Your Constantly Broke Friends/Family

A relationship that is defined by what you put into it materially is not a healthy relationship. Put another way: You can be the most supportive and loving friend, sibling, cousin, et cetera, without ever giving away a penny. Money is not central to any relationship and is not a prerequisite for maintaining a relationship. To think otherwise is to devalue yourself and the relationship— and by now you know you are to never put yourself on sale!

Yet I know this is another vexing commitment for women. We feel so guilty if we are doing better than a financially struggling friend that we agree to cosign a loan or cosign a credit card agreement without weighing the risks to our own financial health. Or when a beloved brother who has already gone through bankruptcy calls to say he needs a $25,000 loan for another ill-fated financial gambit, we say yes, even though the money totally cleans out the cash in our emergency savings account. Or when our cousin calls looking for investors in his new business, we decide to forgo the $4,000 retirement contribution this year so we can help him launch his dream.

Emotionally, every one of those actions makes perfect sense. But emotion doesn't build financial security. You cannot let your heart dominate every decision in your life. You must engage your head, too. It is a delicate balancing act, but so often I see women just let everything fall onto the emotional side of the scale.

A woman who is in touch with the eight qualities will use them to contemplate the financial impact of always saying yes to friends and family in need. Remember, you never want to give money that depletes your financial security. It's that nurturing trait running amok again, so let me repeat: You cannot give if it weakens you.

I would be doubly cautious of anyone who needs your help in getting a loan. You need to realize that lenders love to give out money; it's how they earn a profit. So if a lender sees something in your friend or brother that makes them so nervous they insist on a cosigner, you should be nervous, too. Please understand that when you cosign a loan you are essentially agreeing to pay off the debt if your friend or relative can't. If you are unable to live up to that responsibility, your financial life is going to be a mess. My general advice is never to cosign a loan or a credit card agreement for someone who can't get either on his or her own. It's a clear sign they have problems being financially responsible. And your commitment to them should not rest on your willingness to be their financial backstop.

▲ **I also want you to exercise the same caution with anyone who comes to you for a personal loan. If you must say yes, please treat this for what it really is: a business transaction. On my website are tips for how friends and relatives should draw up a formal loan agreement.**

Perhaps the hardest step to take is to gauge whether your financial help really is a supportive gesture. Loaning money to a sister who is knee-deep in debt because her husband refuses to get a job and keeps tapping their home equity is not as kind and generous as it may at first seem. What your sister really needs is your emotional support to stand up to her husband and insist that they no longer pile on more and more debt. Giving her money doesn't change her husband's behavior. In fact, it might just give her an excuse to avoid the problems in her marriage. It might ultimately be more supportive not to lend money—at least until she takes some steps to address the matter that caused the financial mess in the first place.

You and Your Coworkers

It seems like every week it's someone's birthday/going away party/ engagement party and you're asked to kick in $25 for the party or present. It adds up pretty quickly, and the pinch hurts even more when you don't have that kind of money to give away. But it's embarrassing to refuse—you don't want to be called out for not being a team player. Here, my friend, is where you have to summon your courage to help you to be honest. Simply state the truth: "I just don't have the money this month to spend on the party, but I would love to help out." That's right—offer to help. Be the one who collects the money, shops for the present, goes to the bakery, or circulates the card. Bake cookies for the event. Show you care in a way other than by giving money. Your actions say you care, not your monetary contribution.

When Your Parents Act Like Children

When your parents have always been responsible with money and then something unforeseen happens and they find themselves in a situation where they need your financial help, I will be the first to tell you to go above and beyond the call of duty to be there for them.

On the other hand, if your parents have refused to act like adults and have lived a lifetime of bad spending habits, then it is a whole other situation. If your parents keep asking you for financial help—and even if you can afford it—then you need to step up now and communicate to them that you have love to give them but not financial support. You have a mortgage, student loans from your college days, and now two kids of your own to support. And given that they refuse to grow up, you refuse to take on their financial baggage. What you can offer them is your help in cleaning up their finances so they are in the best possible shape when retirement does arrive. This is not about cutting them out, it is about reaching out. For their own sake and for yours.

Caring for Your Parents

When the time comes for you to assume the role of willing and loving caregiver to your parents, I want to make sure you are fully prepared. That means planning ahead, because it will be very difficult for you to keep your commitments to everyone and everything else you have going on in your life if you haven't. The one thing that will make your life and your parents' lives financially easier is long-term-care insurance. In fact, long-term-care insurance is not just for your parents; it is important for all women approaching the age of fifty-nine.

LONG-TERM CARE INSURANCE

The fact that women live longer than men increases the likelihood that we may at some point be widowed and unable to care for ourselves.

A sobering reality of aging is that one day we may no longer be the wonder women we once were, caring for our parents, our children, our husbands, our friends. One day we may not even be able to care for ourselves. Whether it be a nursing home or at-home care, we may indeed need help. And that's quite expensive.

A health insurance policy will not cover this kind of care. Nor will Medicare in most cases. So who will pay for long-term care if needed? You will—out of your own pocket.

Here is a scenario I want you to avoid: Your mom and dad have worked forever and have diligently saved for retirement. They have about $400,000 in retirement accounts, own their home, and both of them are receiving Social Security payments. They are doing just fine—until your dad becomes ill and needs skilled care that costs about $5,000 a month. In order to afford this, your mom ends up taking about $100,000 a year out of their retirement savings. Four years later, your dad dies. During those four years, your mom has nearly depleted all the money in their retirement accounts, and now there is only one Social Security check coming in. You help to the extent you are able, but still your mom is struggling financially in her so-called golden years. This could have been avoided if you had long-term-care insurance in place for them.

▲ **To get more information on what you need to know about long-term-care insurance, go to my website.**

YOU AND YOUR . . . *FINANCIAL PROFESSIONAL?*

You know that what I want most of all is for you to turn toward your money and get involved with it. I want you to become a saver and then an investor, and I know you have the goods to do it. I'm a pragmatist, however, so I also know that once women—and men—have a significant amount of money, they often choose to hire a financial advisor to manage their money for them.

Entering into a relationship with a financial advisor is right up there among the most important committed relationships you can have. And if you go this route, I will ask you to remain vigilant about doing what is right, rather than what is easy. It is easy never to look at your statements; it *is* easy to follow your advisor's advice blindly—but it is not right. And you cannot break your commitment to yourself. So when you do work with a financial advisor, it is important that you remain vigilant and stay totally involved. The key, however, is finding an advisor worthy of your commitment.

What to Look for in a Financial Advisor

First I want you to be wise to the fact that just about anyone can call themselves a financial advisor; in fact, many so-called advisors are nothing but salespeople dressed up to impress you. I know this firsthand—remember, I got my start as a financial advisor for a major brokerage firm in 1980. I spent most of my training time learning how to sell you the investments they wanted me to sell you. You know what they taught me? Rather than calling you and asking you if you wanted to buy 100 shares of a stock, I was to ask you if you wanted to buy 100 or 200 shares of a stock. What's the difference? If I asked you the first question, you could simply say no. If you said no, then what would I say? But the second question you can't answer with a yes or a no. See what I mean?

Even if an advisor you are considering comes highly recommended by a friend, I need to ask you: Does that friend have a true understanding of how they are doing with their money? Are you sure that they have not been sold a bill of goods? Any advisor you use needs to answer the questions below to my satisfaction.

▲ **How long have you been a financial advisor?** At least ten years is what you want to hear. Experience is an important factor. You want to know that the person giving you advice has been through good and bad economic times.

▲ **What certificates, licenses, or accreditations do you have?** Your advisor has got to be licensed to give you advice. Nobody, and I mean *nobody*, should be giving financial advice in any way, shape, or form if they have not taken the time to get the necessary credentials to give you that advice. At the very least, you want your advisor to have one if not more of the following certifications and licenses:

~ CERTIFIED FINANCIAL PLANNER™ (CFP®)
~ Chartered Financial Consultant (ChFC)
~ Personal Financial Specialist (PFS)
~ NAPFA-Registered Financial Advisor
~ Financial Planning Association (FPA)
~ A Series 7 license
~ A Series 6 license
~ Registered Investment Advisors License

A Word About Credentials

If you are looking for someone to help you in all areas of your financial life—from insurance to taxes to estate planning and from retirement planning to investments—I want you to work with an advisor who is a CERTIFIED FINANCIAL PLAN-NER™, or CFP®. Someone who has taken the time to do the coursework and complete the exams to earn the CFP® designation must also keep up with continuing education credits to keep their certification current.

How Financial Advisors Charge for Their Services

Do not ask a financial advisor what he or she charges. I only want you to work with a financial advisor who tells you exactly how they charge—without your having to ask. This is an important measure of their honesty.

This is how they should charge:

▲ They charge an hourly rate to give you advice.
  or
▲ They charge a percentage of the assets they have under management for you.
  or
▲ A combination of the above.

If they tell you they charge only commissions, do not work with them. Why would you want to work with an advisor who is compensated only when you buy and sell whatever they tell you to buy and sell? When you do this, they make money even if you do not.

If you use an advisor who charges you an hourly rate to give you advice, it could very easily cost you about $1,000 or more. That's why it's my recommendation that you use a financial advisor only if you have $50,000 or more to invest. And if you're thinking that it will cost you less to use an advisor who charges only commissions, I am here to tell you that in most cases you'll be paying a lot more. Let's say you have $50,000 to invest and your financial advisor puts you in a combination of investments that on average has a 5 percent commission. That is $2,500 in commission—a lot more than if you had paid $1,000 to be told what to do.

If you have enough money (usually $50,000 or more), you can seek the services of a money manager or a registered investment advisor. Usually they charge a percentage of the amount of money you have on deposit with them. Under no circumstances should you pay more than a 1 percent fee.

(If you use an advisor who charges an annual fee, please make sure you get good value for your money. I think your advisor should invest your money in either individual stocks or low-cost mutual funds. An advisor who charges an annual fee and then invests your money in loaded mutual funds with high expense ratios is bad news. You will end up paying way too much money in fees. If your advisor recommends mutual funds, they should be no-load mutual funds—or ETFs—with very low expense ratios.)

Not So Fast—Just a Few More Questions

If you were referred to this advisor, did the person referring you get a referral fee?	The answer should be a resounding NO.
Is this advisor currently involved in any lawsuits based on her investment advice? Has she ever been involved in any lawsuits?	Again the answer should be a big NO; if it's yes, ask her to explain why.

Has this advisor ever had disciplinary actions taken against her?	Another NO here, but if she answers yes, have her explain why.
What is her expertise?	You want to hear that she can provide you with advice on all matters having to do with money, from estate planning to getting out of debt.
Will you receive quarterly updates of your financial accounts and an annual year-end report?	The answer you want to hear is YES.
Will those reports show your actual rate of return, net of the money you invested over the year?	YES again!
Will she ever ask you to make out an investment check directly to her, in her name?	NO, NO, NO. You are to never sign over money to an individual; your money is to be invested directly in your account at the brokerage or fund company you will be using. Never entrust your money to any single person.

Does she ask you questions about your debt?	The answer should be YES.
Does she ask if you have a will or a trust?	YES again.
Does she ask about your health?	Another YES.
Does she ask if you want to buy a home? Or about your mortgage, if you have one?	YES.
Does she ask about your kids?	YES.
Does she ask about the stability of your job?	YES.
Does she ask if you are afraid to invest? How much money you are willing to lose?	She should ask both of these questions.
Does she ask if you are in a good relationship?	The answer should be YES—this is important for her to know.

Did she come to see you?	The answer should be NO— a good advisor would make you come into the office so you can see where she works.
Is her office neat?	It should be. Remember, if the advisor is disorganized, that could be a reflection of how your money will be handled.
Do you like her staff?	You should like all the people who will be working with you and your accounts.
Did the advisor make it mandatory that you come with your spouse or life partner?	YES. A good advisor would never just meet with you alone if you are part of a couple.
Did she explain things in a way that you completely understood?	The answer has to be YES.
Did she try to sell you a variable annuity, variable, universal, or whole-life insurance policy?	NO, NO, NO! If she did, leave immediately.

MAKE ME A PROMISE

Promise me that if you decide to hire a financial advisor you will still stay involved with your money. Remember, even the most talented and best-intentioned advisor will never be as intimately and passionately connected to the growth and care of your money as the woman staring back at you in the mirror.

Your greatest commitment must be to yourself. That is where this whole book is leading you. Look at the woman in the mirror, say her name, and make a pledge to take care of her with your whole heart and soul. She deserves your commitment most of all.

8

SAY YOUR NAME

As this book ends, we draw closer to the moment when you will go off on your own into your new world of money. I want you to see this as a celebratory moment. I want you to celebrate who you are and broadcast it powerfully to the world. Take credit for who you are, what you believe in, what you have achieved, and all that you hope to achieve. There's just one last lesson I have to impart before you go.

As I travel around the country speaking to women's groups, I've noticed something very telling. At some point, the organizer of the event will take a moment to thank a few women in the audience for their work or for their efforts supporting the group over the past year. What typically happens is that the organizer asks these women to stand up as their name is called, and everyone applauds. I watch these women stand . . . well, sort of stand; they rise a little way out of their seats and then sit back down so quickly that if you blinked, you'd miss the whole thing. They want to duck back out of sight as fast as possible. Stop the applause! They can't bear the thought of standing up to receive credit and appreciation for their work.

Is it humility that makes women shy away from praise when their name is spoken out loud?

I have to tell you, I wouldn't call it humility. Actually, it's more like humiliating. You insult yourself and your own efforts when you back off of your accomplishments and therefore your power. It is the exact opposite of what a wealthy woman would do. Ladies, we haven't come this far in the book to allow this terrible trait to persist. I am going to help you to break this habit, because it's more corrosive, way more damaging to your whole self, than you are willing to believe.

WHAT'S IN A NAME?

Think about this. When I ask women to state their name, do you know what they say to me? They say which name? My maiden name, my married name, or my divorced name? When my mom got married, she became Mrs. Morris Orman. What happened to her first name, her last name? They were gone forever within a few vows. My dad died more than twenty-five years ago, and yet to this day mail comes addressed to Mrs. Morris Orman. My dad never had to think about whether he would keep his birth name or change it to his wife's last name, or do a hyphenated combination of both. Men never have to think about that, but even today, it is still a question that gets put to every woman, young or old, who is about to marry—or remarry. Are you going to change your name? It's hard not to see the persistence of this tradition as an unspoken agreement in our society that a woman's name is not as important as a man's.

As for me, I never thought my name would matter. I was born Susan Lynn Orman. But to my family and friends, I was always Susie. I thought Susie was a plain name that didn't match my adventurous spirit. I wanted to be different from everyone else. I wanted to change my name, but I didn't want to hurt my mom's feelings. When I was in college, I came up with a plan to change the spelling of my name to S U Z E. I thought it was cool and different, and best of all, my mom would never know about it, because when would she ever see my name in print? *Who knew?* To this day, she has never asked me why I changed the spelling of my name, because to her I will always just be her Susie. Don't you love that?

But time always has a way of putting things right back to where they started. Let me explain. My mother, as I write this, is ninety-one years of age and has for a few years now lived in an independent-living facility for seniors. Whenever I go to visit her, she introduces me to everyone as her daughter, and then she tells them with great pride what I do, since that is what she thinks is important for her friends to know about me. Her friends will then look at me and say, "And what is your name?" But when my mom introduces her friends to me, she doesn't tell me what they did for a living, she simply introduces them by name. "Suze, this is Anne Travis and this is Thelma Notkin." Clearly, there comes a time in our lives when what we have or what we have done does not matter to anyone anymore. The only thing that matters is our name.

Are you thinking, *Nice story, Suze, but what does that have to do with women and money?* Why is the final chapter of this book called "Say Your Name"?

I believe that there is something incredibly powerful in the act of saying your name. I might even go as far as to say that it is the symbolic key to unlocking your powerful self. I believe that it is not until you can say your name with pride, incredible pride for who you are and all that your name represents, that you will ever be the powerful woman I want you to be. And I don't want you to wait until you are ninety-one years of age to do so.

Now Is the Time to Say Your Name: An Exercise

What name do you want to announce to the world as yours? Your birth name, your married name? You decide, but it must be your full name, not just your first name. Next, I want you to practice something that you may never have done in your life. First, stand before a mirror. I want you to look into the mirror and, as you look at yourself, say your name. Your full name. Watch your face as you say it. Listen to your voice as you say it. I want you to be aware of your body as you say it. Go on, try this right now.

As you are doing this, I want you to take note of how you feel. Do you feel shy? Do you feel foolish? Are you finding it hard not to laugh at your image? What's your body language like? Do you want to cover your face, or wrap your arms around your body to make yourself smaller? Or are you standing tall, with your head held high? Or maybe your arms are crossed defensively. Do you feel strong and powerful? Hmm, my guess is probably not.

I ask you now to recall the eight qualities of a wealthy woman. Remember the courage it takes to speak your mind. Remember that your thoughts, feelings, words, and actions should be one. Are they in harmony when you are talking about yourself? What are you thinking, what are you doing when you say your name?

Now step a few feet away from the mirror. I'm going to ask you to try this again, except this time I want you first to imagine that you are about to walk onto a stage with 30,000 people waiting to hear what you have to say. I want you to know that everyone out there wants to hear what you have to say. They have paid good money for their seats, and you are the sole reason they are there. I'm going to ask you to look in the mirror and, with all the support and love of those

30,000 people behind you, I want you to introduce yourself to this audience with a force like you have never felt before. I'm going to ask you to tell them who you are. What is it you want them to know about you? Think about it for a few minutes, and when you are ready, say it as you are looking in the mirror.

I want you to feel your power. I want you to know what it feels like to present yourself with confidence and clarity. I want you to appreciate how it feels just to say your name as if the whole world wanted to know who you are and what you are all about.

Please try this, don't shy away from it, and even if the only thing you utter today is your name, I want you to do it with all the power that resides within you. Come back to the mirror again and again until you can look yourself directly in the eye and say your name without flinching and without apology.

I want you to understand that simply saying your name is an act of power.

OWNING THE POWER TO CONTROL YOUR DESTINY

This is what I believe with all my heart and soul: Who you are will always be the foundation of what you have in this life. It is one of the goals of this book—and all my life's work—to convince you of that. Who you are is where it all begins. If you want to own the power to control your destiny, there is no other starting place.

We still live in a time that presents us with obstacles to overcome simply because of our gender. But these are not insurmountable obstacles, not at all. And they cannot deter you from your course. Is it going to be easy? Well, it depends on how you look at it. You can choose to make this travel plan hard, or you can choose to take it on with all the courage and determination that a powerful woman has within her, and suddenly it's not so hard after all. To your great surprise, you may even find it easy.

Nevertheless, there are bound to be moments when life gets difficult. At these times, as ever, I would ask you to review the eight qualities of a wealthy woman once more.

Remember to muster up your courage and silence your fear.

Remember to keep your eye on the goal, on what you really want to accomplish, no matter what anyone says or does to deter you. Just keep moving ahead.

Remember to stay involved with your money, to nurture a healthy relationship with it, for what happens to your money affects the quality of your life and the lives of all those you love.

Remember always to do what is right rather than what is easy, and never to put yourself on sale, because you deserve better than that.

Last but not least, I ask you to look everyone you meet straight in the eye and with the force and power of all the women in the world behind you, within you, and in front of you, SAY YOUR NAME.

And I am,
Suze Orman

INDEX

ABOUT THE AUTHOR

SUZE ORMAN is the author of five consecutive *New York Times* bestsellers: *The 9 Steps to Financial Freedom*; *The Courage to Be Rich*; *The Road to Wealth*; *The Laws of Money, The Lessons of Life*; and *The Money Book for the Young, Fabulous & Broke*; and the national bestsellers *You've Earned It, Don't Lose It* and *Suze Orman's Financial Guidebook*. She is the host of her own award-winning CNBC-TV show, which airs every Saturday night, and also hosts the *Financial Freedom Hour* on QVC television. She is a contributing editor to *O, The Oprah Magazine* and is a featured writer on Yahoo! Personal Finance with her biweekly Money Matters series.

Orman has written, co-produced, and hosted five PBS specials based on her bestselling books, which have made her the single most successful fundraiser in the history of public television. She has won two Emmy Awards for Outstanding Service Host in 2003 and 2006. She has been honored with three American Women in Radio and Television Gracie Allen Awards, which recognizes the nation's best radio, television, and cable programming for, by, and about women, and in 2003 was inducted into the Books for a Better Life Award Hall of Fame in recognition of her ongoing contributions to self-improvement.

A CERTIFIED FINANCIAL PLANNER™ professional, Orman directed the Suze Orman Financial Group from 1987 to 1997, served as Vice-President-Investments for Prudential-Bache Securities from 1983 to 1987, and was an account executive at Merrill Lynch from 1980 to 1983. A highly sought-after public speaker worldwide, she has been called "a one-woman financial advice powerhouse" in *USA Today* and was profiled in *Worth* magazine's hundredth issue as among those who have "revolutionized the way America thinks about money." She lives in south Florida.